A Brief History of the King's Royal Rifle Corps 1755-1915

A Brief History of the King's Royal Rifle Corps 1755-1915

Sir Edward Hutton

LEONAUR

A Brief History of the King's Royal Rifle Corps 1755-1915
by Sir Edward Hutton

First published under the title
A Brief History of the King's Royal Rifle Corps

Leonaur is an imprint of Oakpast Ltd

ISBN: 978-0-85706-828-6 (hardcover)
ISBN: 978-0-85706-829-3 (softcover)

http://www.leonaur.com

Publisher's Notes

Contents

CELER ET AUDAX.

"Louisberg," "Quebec, 1759," "Martinique, 1762," "Havannah," "North America, 1763-4," "Rolica," "Vimiera," "Martinique, 1809," "Talavera," "Busaco," "Fuentes d'Onor," "Albuhera," "Ciudad Rodrigo," "Badajoz," 'Salamanca," "Vittoria," "Pyrenees," "Nivelle," "Nive," "Orthes," "Toulouse," "Peninsula," "Mooltan," "Goojerat," "Punjaub," "South Africa, 1851-2-3," "Delhi, 1857," "Taku Forts," "Pekin, 1860," "South Africa, 1879," "Ahmad Khel," "Kandahar, 1880," "Afghanistan, 1878-80," "Te!-el-Kebir," "Egypt, 1882, 1884," "Chitral," "Defence of Ladysmith," "Relief of Ladysmith," "South Africa, 1899-1902."

Colonel in Chief:
His Majesty the King.

Colonels Commandant:

1st Battalion Field-Marshal Rt. Hon. F.W. Lord Grenfell, P.C, G.C.B., G.C.M.G.

2nd   ,,   Lieutenant-General Sir Edward T. H. Hutton, K.C.B, K.C.M.G., *p.s.c.*

3rd   ,,   Major-General R. S. R. Fetherstonhaugh, C.B.

4th   ,,   Major-General Sir Wykeham Leigh-Peniberton K.C.B.

Preface

The first edition of this abridged history of the Regiment was in part prepared by certain members of the History Committee, edited by the Chairman, and published in 1912. The first edition of 7,500 copies having been exhausted, a second edition, bringing the history up to the 31st December, 1915, is now published at the request of the General Committee of the *Celer et Audax* Club.

The Editor, Chairman of the History Committee (Lieut.-General Sir Edward Hutton), is indebted to the following members of the Regimental History Committee:—Major-General Astley Terry, Brigadier-General the Hon. C Sackville-West, Lieut.-Colonel Sir Hereward Wake, and also to Brigadier-General Horatio Mends for the contribution, wholly or in part, of Part 1, Pgh 3; Part 2, Pgh. 4 and 5; Part 3, Pgh. 9 and 10; and Part 3, Pgh. 7 and 8 respectively. Colonel Lewis Butler, author of *The Annals of the Regiment*, and Colonel R. Byron, D.S.O., editor of the *Regimental Chronicle*, have also lent their valuable assistance. The editor holds himself alone responsible for the opinions given, and for the deductions drawn.

Every effort has been made to narrate in a concise and popular form the origin, history, and world-wide services of the several battalions, so that every Rifleman may be able to learn at least the outlines of the history of his Regiment—a Corps whose battle honours are unequalled in number, and whose reputation for discipline and courage is unsurpassed in the annals of the British Army.

As Paragraph 10 (South African War, 1899-1902) and Paragraph 12 (Present Great War, August 4th, 1914, to December 31st, 1915) deal with contemporaneous history, and concern members of the Regiment still serving, (as at time of first publication), it has been deemed advisable to adopt a short record of events by battalions, leaving to the historian of the Regiment the compilation hereafter of the complete narrative.

The gallant exploits of the Regiment are here given in no spirit of pride or self-adulation, but with the earnest hope that, profiting by the example of their predecessors, the present and future generations of Riflemen may not only successfully maintain as a sacred trust the credit and renown of The King's Royal Rifle Corps, but may also still further add to the honours and reputation already won.

The editor.

December 31st, 1916.

SPECIAL NOTE.

The names of Officers of the British Army who are alluded to, and who do not belong to the Regiment, are printed in italics.

1

1755-1763.—Origin of the Regiment and its Services in North America, as 60th Royal Americans

The Regiment was raised during 1755-56 in North America under special conditions—Christmas Day, 1755, has always been adopted as the actual birthday—for the express purpose of assisting our Army to retrieve the terrible disaster which had befallen the British troops under *General Braddock* on the 8th July, 1755, at the hands of a smaller force of French and Red Indians in the forest fastnesses upon the banks of the Ohio River. It had been found that the slow and ponderous movements of troops trained upon the German model, with their heavy accoutrements, tight uniforms, and unsuitable tactics, were helpless against savages, and almost equally helpless against soldiers such as those of France then serving in America, who were habituated to war in the dense forests and trackless wastes of that country. It was therefore decided by the British Government to raise in America, from the Colonists themselves, a force which should be able to meet these conditions.

Designated as the 62nd, and the following year as the 60th Royal Americans, the Regiment was accordingly formed of 4,000 men in four battalions, and General The Earl of Loudoun, Commander-in-Chief of the British Army in America, was appointed Colonel-in-Chief. It was recruited from settlers, mainly of German and Swiss origin, in the States of Massachusetts, New York, Pennsylvania, Maryland, and North Carolina, to which were added volunteers from British regiments and others from Europe. Many of the senior officers and a considerable number of the company officers were also drawn from the armies of Europe, some of them being highly trained and experienced soldiers.

Through the bold initiative of Lieutenant-Colonel Henry Bouquet,[1] a Swiss officer of distinction, commanding the 1st Battalion, the 60th Royal Americans adopted Colonial methods of equipment, simpler drill, open formations, and the Indian system of forest warfare, thus early acquiring those attributes of individual action, swift initiative, and of elastic though firm discipline, which have been the conspicuous characteristics of the Regiment throughout its long and brilliant career, characteristics which have made its reputation. Thus equipped, The Royal American Regiment from its very beginning played a distinguished and memorable part in establishing British power in North America.

The great struggle between France and England for supremacy in America was at its height, when early in 1758, Abercromby,[2] who had succeeded Loudoun as commander-in-chief, decided upon a general advance. The plan of campaign was to invade Canada on two fronts—one from the South, *via* Lake Champlain, plain, upon Montreal and the Western portion of Canada, and the other from the East by sea, *via* Louisburg (Cape Breton) and the St. Lawrence River, upon Quebec and the Eastern.

The 1st and 4th Battalions, under Bouquet and Haldimand,[3] formed part of the main Army in the Western Field of operations, and on the banks of Lake Champlain, at the memorable defeat of Ticonderoga, (July 8th), "at once a glory and a shame," the 4th Battalion and a portion of the 1st showed a stubborn courage worthy of the highest praise, and lost very heavily in killed and wounded. On July the 27th,

---

1 .Afterwards Brigadier-General Bouquet. Born 1719, died 1766. The victor of Bushey Run. A brilliant officer, of the highest capacity as a leader and administrator. It has been said that by his untimely death Great Britain lost a general whose presence might well have caused the American War of Independence to assume a different aspect. *Vide* Biographical sketch, *Regimental Chronicle*, 1910, also Bouquet MS., British Museum. *Bouquet & the Ohio Indian War* by Cyrus Cort and William Smith, two accounts of the campaigns of 1763-64, also published by Leonaur.
2. General James Abercromby, Colonel-in-Chief, 1767-1768.
3. Afterwards Lieut.-General Sir Frederick Haldimand. Born 1710, died 1791. Like his friend and comrade. Colonel Bouquet, he was a Swiss soldier of fortune. In his earlier career he served under Frederick the Great, and was present at the battle of Mollwitz. Commander-in-Chief in North America, and Governor of Canada—he was a distinguished soldier and civil administrator. *Vide Haldimand Papers*, British Museum; also *Life of Sir F. Haldimand*, "Makers of Canada "series (Toronto, 1904).

three weeks later, regardless of their losses, the Regiment furnished a part of the column under Bradstreet,[4] of the 60th, which, after a forced march, captured Fort Frontenac on Lake Ontario by a *coup de main* upon the 27th August.

In November following the 1st Battalion, employed on the Western frontiers under *General Forbes*, played the leading part in the advance against Fort Duquesne on the Ohio, and led by the gallant Bouquet effected its capture from the French and Red Indians, (November 25th). This brilliant triumph over great physical difficulties was achieved by sheer determination, endurance, and pluck; and the solid value of the victory is thus summed up by the American historian, Parkman:—

> It opened the great West to English enterprise, took from France half her savage allies, and relieved her Western borders from the scourge of Indian Wars.

Fort Duquesne, re-christened Fort Pitt, was thereupon garrisoned by a detachment of the 60th, and was destined later to play a prominent part in the subsequent operations.

The 2nd and 3rd Battalions, under Lieut.-Colonel Young and Major Augustine Prevost[5] respectively, early in 1758 were ordered to join Generals Amherst[6] and *Wolfe* in the Eastern Field of operations, and they took a prominent part in the landing and capture of Louisburg, (July 26th), the great stronghold and sea-base of the French at Cape Breton.

These two battalions were subsequently in 1759 moved up the St. Lawrence to Quebec, where they still further distinguished themselves at Montmorency Falls, below Quebec, on July the 31st, and by their rapid movements and their intrepid courage won from *General Wolfe* the motto of *"Celer et Audax"* (*Swift and Bold*). A still greater opportunity occurred on the 13th of September at the decisive battle of Quebec, where upon the Plains of Abraham the 2nd Battalion, whose light company covering the landing had been the first to scale the heights, protected the left during the battle against a very superior

---

4. Afterwards Major-General John Bradstreet. Born 1710, died 1774; a successful leader of irregular troops. Greatly distinguished himself at Ticonderoga and Oswego.
5. Afterwards Major General. Swiss by extraction, he was born 1723, and died 1786; dangerously wounded in July, 1759, above Quebec; the victor of Savannah, 1779, and a distinguished soldier.
6. Afterwards Field-Marshal Sir Jeffery Amherst, Baron Amherst, Colonel-in-Chief, 1758-1797.

force of Red Indians and French, who made the most determined efforts to assail the flank and rear of *Wolfe's* army under cover of the dense bush and rocky ground. The Grenadier Companies of the 2nd and 3rd Battalions were included in the companies, comprising the Louisburg Grenadiers—a *corps d'elite*—to whom was assigned the place of honour in the centre of the Line. It was in close proximity to our grenadiers that the immortal *Wolfe* fell, and it is said that it was Lieutenant John Brown, of The Royal Americans, who was the first to reach the dying hero, and, together with Lieutenant J. F.W. des Barres,[7] his A.D.C, also of the Regiment, to raise him from the ground. The 3rd Battalion played a no less important part by holding in check the enemy under Bougainville, who threatened the rear through the thick woods on the river bank.

The Regiment had thus a prominent share in this momentous victory—which gave the possession of the North American Continent finally to the Anglo-Saxon race.

Amherst, who in 1759 had succeeded Abercromby in chief command of the Army, led the main force in its advance to Montreal, where, on the 8th of September, 1760, the 4th Battalion, a portion of the 1st, and the Grenadiers of the 2nd and 3rd, shared in the glories of the surrender of the French Army under the Marquis de Vaudreuil— a surrender through which the supremacy in America finally passed to the British Crown.

Following up their successes in 1758 under *General Forbes* in 1760—1763. the Ohio Valley, Bouquet and the 1st Battalion had by degrees captured or occupied the whole of the French posts west of the Alleghany Mountains, and they were accordingly chosen for the arduous task of defending the various forts established in the unexplored country south of the great lakes. A region embracing thousands of square miles of dense forest and immense lakes was thus consigned to the keeping of five or six hundred men—a vast responsibility for a single weak Battalion garrisoning a few insignificant forts.

In 1763 took place the general and sudden rising of the Indians under Pontiac—a formidable conspiracy, bringing ruin and desolation to the settlers in those wild regions, and even threatening the safety of the Colonies themselves. By surprise or stratagem the Indians, in overwhelming numbers, secured many of the widely scattered

---

7. Afterwards Major-General. Born 1722, died 1824. An engineer of Huguenot birth; he assisted to navigate the Fleet up the St. Lawrence; became Governor of Prince Edward's Island, and died aged 102.

posts held by the 60th, murdering some of the slender garrisons and beleaguering others. But the important posts of Fort Detroit upon the Straits joining Lake Erie and Lake Huron, and of Fort Pitt commanding the Ohio River valley, both garrisoned by the 60th under Gladwyn[8] and Ecuyer respectively, were gallantly and successfully held against tremendous odds. The relief of these two important posts were operations of the greatest urgency, and every effort was made to get sufficient troops for this purpose.

It was at once decided that Fort Pitt on the Ohio, guarding as it did the Western frontier of the Colonies, must be saved at any cost, but owing to the reduction of the Army in America after the great war, it was with the utmost difficulty that, at Carlisle, 150 miles west of Philadelphia, a small column was formed under Bouquet, consisting of barely 500 men of the 1st Battalion 60th Royal Americans and the 42nd Highlanders. This courageous band, led by the stout-hearted and experienced Henry Bouquet, marched almost as a forlorn hope to the relief of the garrison. Reaching, after a long and weary march, the dangerous defiles of Bushey Run, twenty miles from their objective and Aug. 5th and 6th, within view of the scene of Braddock's crushing defeat, a site of battle deliberately chosen by their cunning foe, the little force was suddenly attacked by a vastly superior force of Indian braves.

During two long trying days the combatants fought a desperate battle, until at last Bouquet's genius as a leader achieved a brilliant victory. The fight becoming stagnant and his men showing signs of exhaustion. Bouquet saw that the crisis had come, and adopted a ruse often practised by the Indians themselves of assuming a retreat and withdrawing a portion of the front, and thus inducing his opponents to attack.

The stratagem succeeded, and Bouquet delivered a desperate counter-attack upon the fronts and flanks simultaneously, of the enemy thus caught in the open, which completely routed the stubborn foe. This victory, pronounced by an American historian "the best contested action ever fought between white men and Indians," was followed up in the coming year by a vigorous advance by Bradstreet upon Detroit by way of Lake Erie; and by Bouquet marching from Fort Pitt with a column consisting of his own battalion of the 60th, the 42nd, and Pro-

---

8. Major Gladwyn was promoted from the 80th Regiment into the 60th Royal Americans in 1762, but was re-transferred later to his old Regiment.—(Bouquet MSS., British Museum.)

vincial troops, which he led into the very heart of the enemy's country. Bouquet's column was triumphant, and upon reaching the Indian settlements on the River Muskingum, deep in the wild fastnesses of the primeval forest, their leader's diplomatic skill and defiant attitude completed the successful issue of the campaign. Bouquet thus rightly earned for himself and his men the credit of having finally broken the French influence and Red Indian power in the West, giving to the British Crown all the vast territories west of the Alleghany Mountains and south of the Great Lakes, comprising now the States of Pennsylvania, Virginia, Western Virginia, Ohio, Kentucky, Indiana, Michigan, and Illinois, (November 15th, 1764, Red Indian Campaign).

The conspicuous part played at this period by the 60th Royal Americans, and the exceptional merit of many of its officers have hitherto been better understood in the United States and in Canada than by our own countrymen. But it is now at last acknowledged that the Regiment, owing to its especial attributes, was in the forefront of all those operations which (more than any others) added a peculiar lustre to the British Crown at this early stage of the evolution of the British Empire in North America. There is no period in its eventful history of which The King's Royal Rifle Corps may more justly be proud than the epoch from its birth in 1755 to the final overthrow of the French and Red-Indian power in 1764.

The dominating influence in the Regiment at this period was undoubtedly Henri Bouquet. His spirit of initiative and his force of character caused reforms, which he had introduced into the 60th Royal Americans, both of organization, drill, tactics, and equipment to be adopted by the whole Army.

Meanwhile, in 1761, the 3rd Battalion, under Augustine Prevost, moving to the West Indies, had taken part in the first capture of Martinique from the French on the 27th January, 1762. It subsequently joined the expedition to Cuba under the *Earl of Albemarle,* where, led by Brigadier-General Haviland,[9] it played a leading part in the capture of Havannah from the Spaniards on the 13th of August, in the course of which it penetrated into a morass, where it charged and defeated a regiment of Spanish dragoons and other mounted troops.

9. Afterwards General William Haviland: Colonel Commandant 1761-1762.

2

1764—1807.—West Indies and the
American War

On the termination of the French War in America the British Army was reduced, and in 1764 and 1763 respectively the 3rd and 4th Battalions were disbanded. The discontented and hostile feeling of the American Colonies at this period rendered it advisable to transfer The Royal Americans to the West Indies, recruited as they were from the Colonists themselves. Thus it fell to the lot of the Regiment to take a prominent share in the conquest and annexation of the West Indian Islands and the adjacent coast, which took place at this period. The officers in many instances filled important posts as Governors and Administrators of the various islands. On the outbreak of the War of Independence in 1775 the 3rd and 4th Battalions were again raised in England and despatched to the West Indies, and thence to Florida, where they figured prominently in the operations in that region.

In 1779 the 3rd and some companies of the 4th Battalion formed portion of an army under General Augustine Prevost in Georgia and South Carolina. The Regiment played a leading part at the brilliant action of Briars Creek (March 3rd, 1779), and also in the subsequent siege of Savannah, where a superior force of French and Americans under Comte d'Estaigne and General Lincoln was successfully held at bay by a very much smaller army under Prevost, and at the final assault was signally defeated with great loss (October the 9th, 1779).

An improvised body of Light Dragoons (or Mounted Infantry), organised by Lieut.-Colonel Marc Prevost,[1] of the 60th, did remark-

---

1. Lieut.-Colonel Marc Prevost, born 1736, died 1785, youngest brother of General Augustine Prevost—a brilliant and most promising officer, who succumbed to the effect of his wounds.

able service during these operations, and at the victory on the 9th of October lost heavily, but greatly distinguished itself by repulsing the main assaulting column of the enemy and capturing the colour of the Carolina Regiment, now in the possession of the Prevost family.

Upon the termination of the American War of Independence in 1783 the 3rd and 4th Battalions were disbanded for the second time, but were again raised in 1788 for the third time and despatched to the West Indies. The 1st and 2nd Battalions at this period were quietly stationed in Canada until in 1797 a partial reconstruction took place.

The 3rd and 4th Battalions in the West Indies took part in the following military operations at this period:—

Capture of Nicaragua-Panama	April 13th,	1780
Capture by assault of the Island of Tobago, a brilliant feat of arms	April 17th,	1783
Capture (2nd) of Martinique	March 23rd,	1794
„ Saint Lucia	April 2nd,	1794
„ Grande Terre Guadaloupe	April 12th,	1794
„ Saint Vincent	June 9th,	1796
„ Trinidad	Feb. 18th,	1797
Attack on Porto Rico	April 18th,	1797
Capture (3rd) of Martinique	Feb. 24th,	1809

It will be seen that the Regiment at this period was closely identified with the ebb and flow of disaster and success in the conquest and re-conquest of the West Indian Islands. It was cursed with a perpetual and deplorable death-rate due to disease, official negligence or ignorance, and the vicissitudes of the notoriously evil climate. Yet the spirit of the Regiment, which had won from Wolfe himself the proud motto of "*Celer et Audax*," remained—the spirit of the original heroes of Louisburg, of Ticonderoga, of Quebec, of Bushey Run, and of Savannah still survived! On the 23rd of August, 1797, Field-Marshal H.R.H. Frederick Duke of York[2] was appointed Colonel-in-Chief of the Regiment, *vice* Lord Amherst deceased.

In December of the same year the famous 5th Battalion was raised at Cowes, Isle of Wight, under Lieutenant-Colonel Baron Francis de Rottenburg,[3] upon the Austrian model as a Special Corps of *Jäagers* or

---

2. Frederick, Duke of York, was the second son of George III, and brother of George IV and William IV.

3. Afterwards Lieutenant-General. Born 1760, died 1832. He commanded the 5th Battalion, 1797-1808. An Austrian by birth, and ancestry.

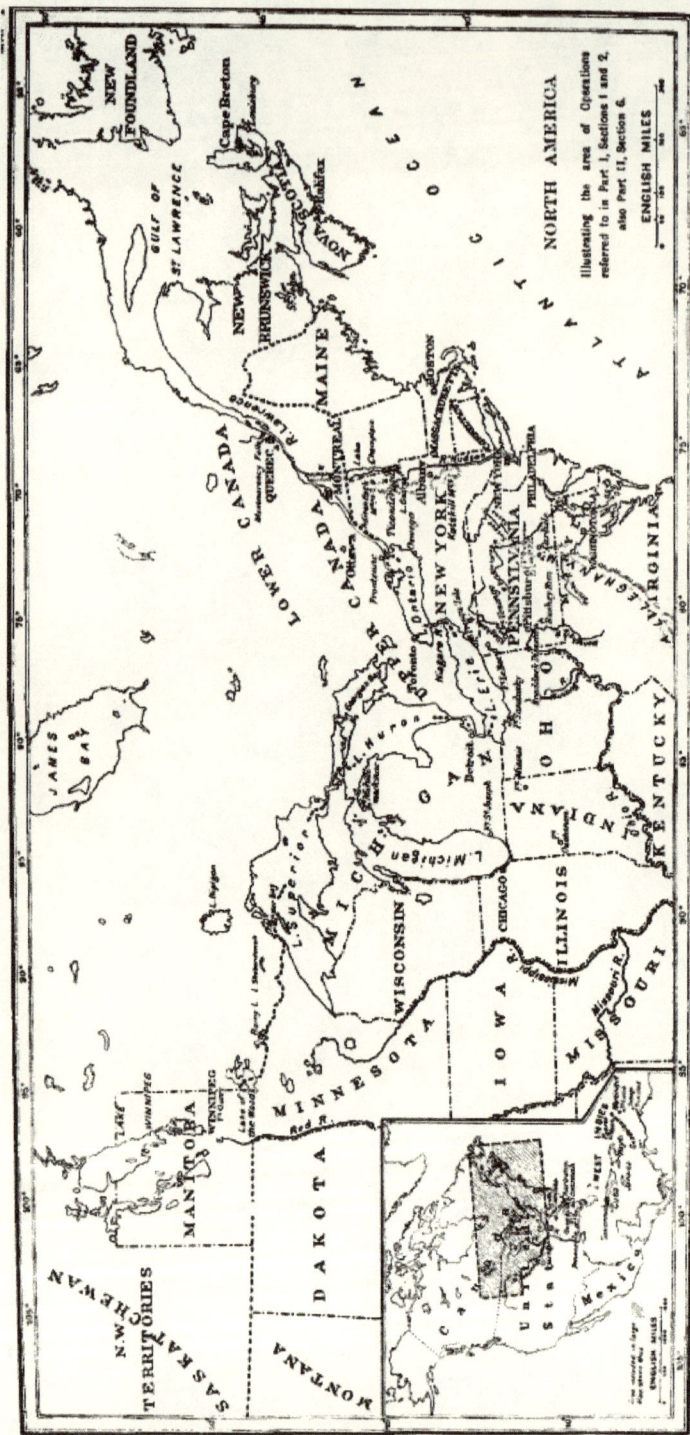

MAP 1 NORTH AMERICA

Riflemen. Four hundred of Hompesch's Mounted Riflemen—a German Corps raised for service under the British Crown—were drafted into the battalion, which was armed with rifles and dressed in green with red facings.

The second lieutenant-colonel was that celebrated Robert Crauford, who afterwards made his name so famous in the Peninsular War as the honoured leader of the Light Division. Thus, by the addition of the 5th Battalion to the Regiment as Riflemen in 1797, the gradual evolution of the 60th Royal Americans into The King's Royal Rifle Corps was auspiciously begun.

The raising of this battalion and the appointment of Lieut.-Colonel Francis de Rottenburg to its command, marks not only a distinct epoch in the history of the Regiment, but an important stage in the development of the British Army.

Just as Bouquet in 1756 had introduced radical changes of dress and tactics into the newly-raised 60th Royal Americans in America, and thus into the British Army, so also did De Rottenburg in 1797 introduce a system of Riflemen and Light Infantrymen's duties new to the British Army, which contributed not a little to the successful issue of the Peninsula campaign.

De Rottenburg prepared for Field-Marshal H.R.H. Duke of
1798-1808. York—recently appointed Commander-in-Chief—the
Regulations for the Exercise of Riflemen and Light Infantry, and Instructions for their conduct in the Field, illustrated by excellent diagrams, which, with a memo, by the adjutant-general, was published in 1798. This book proved the text-book for the training of the 5th Battalion, and was thereupon adopted for use in the British Army; it formed the basis upon which subsequent Rifle and Light Infantry battalions were organised and trained. It was this work which largely influenced the illustrious Lieutenant-General Sir John Moore, who in regard to his training of the famous Light Division, thus writes to the adjutant-general (August 30th, 1803):—

I mean to make De Rottenburg the ground-work, noting in the margin whatever changes we make from him.

It is interesting to record that in 1788 Sir John Moore himself served as major in the 60th Royal Americans, and that De Rottenburg in 1808 succeeded him at Shorncliffe and Brabourne as a trainer of the Light Troops of the British Army.

In 1799 a 6th Battalion was added to the Regiment—a company

of which was clothed and trained as a Rifle company—so that the
close of the eighteenth century saw the Regiment composed of six
battalions.

3

1808-1824.—Peninsular War, 60th The Royal American Regiment becomes 60th The Duke of York's Own Rifle Corps

In 1808 Great Britain determined to take the offensive against France, and, by occupying Portugal, endeavoured to drive Napoleon and the French from the Peninsula of Spain and Portugal.

Thus began the Peninsular War, so full of glorious memories for the British Army. The 5th Battalion, under the command of Major Davy,[1] formed part of the force despatched under *Sir Arthur Wellesley* to Portugal, and in conjunction with the 2nd Battalion of the 95th [2] opened the campaign at Obidos on the 15th of August; and two days later took part in the fight of Roleia. The services of the battalion as Light Troops or Riflemen were valued so highly by the commander of the forces, and so important was their example, that in a very complimentary order he directed its distribution by companies among the several brigades of the army. Thus it came to be engaged in nearly all the great battles throughout the war, starting brilliantly with the Battle of Vimiera,[3] (August 21st, 1808), where a signal victory was gained over the French under General Junot.

Wellesley was shortly afterwards superseded by Sir Harry Burrard [4]

1. Afterwards General Sir William Gabriel Davy, C.B., K.C.H., Colonel Commandant, 60th Rifles, 1842-1856. He succeeded Baron de Rottenburg in command of the 5th Battalion in 1808.
2. Formed in 1800, and now The Rifle Brigade.
3. The battalion was especially mentioned in Wellesley's despatch.
4. Formerly a captain in the 60th.

and *Sir Hew Dalrymple*, who ended the campaign by the Convention of Cintra, under the terms of which the French evacuated Portugal.

The three commanders were then ordered home, and Sir John Moore [5] was selected to advance with a force upon Madrid. *Sir David Baird* landed at Corunna with reinforcements, including the 2nd Battalion, and on the 20th of December he joined Moore near Mayorgo. By the masterly dispositions of Napoleon himself, an overwhelming force of French was concentrated under Marshal Soult, which forced the British to retire on Corunna. Soult, following in pursuit, attacked them in the act of embarking, but met with a crushing defeat. The British, however, paid a high price for their victory: *Baird* was severely wounded, and the gallant Sir John Moore was killed— his death being a heavy loss to the British Army. At this juncture General Hope [6] took over the command and completed the embarkation of the troops. The 2nd Battalion, having been allotted to the defence of the town of Corunna, was in part only engaged in the battle, (January 16th, 1809).

In 1809 *Wellesley*, for the second time, landed in Portugal and assumed command. He at once advanced against Soult, who had invaded the northern provinces, and by a brilliant feat of arms forced the passage of the River Douro, and drove Soult out of Portugal. Then, marching upon Madrid by the valley of the Tagus, he defeated the French at Talavera, (July 27th and 28th). In his subsequent despatches Sir Arthur spoke warmly of our Regiment, which deserved his praise, for by its smartness and intrepidity it had saved him from being taken prisoner. "Upon this occasion," he states in his despatch, "the steadiness and discipline of the 5th Battalion 60th Regiment were conspicuous."

The French having been largely reinforced, *Wellesley* retired into Portugal, which was invaded in 1810 by the enemy under Marshal Massena. The British General, now created Lord Wellington, inflicted on the French a sanguinary check at Busaco, (September 27th), where the 60th—under Colonel Williams[7]—again distinguished themselves. The enemy was, however, too strong to be permanently stopped, and Wellington retired to the lines of Torres Vedras, covering Lisbon.

Thence, in 1811, he again advanced; expelled the French from Portugal, and defeated them at Fuentes d'Onor, (May 3rd and 5th). A

---

5. Formerly major in the 4th Battalion 60th.

6. Afterwards General The Earl of Hopetoun, G.C.B., Colonel Commandant 6th Battalion 60th.

7. Afterwards Major-General Sir William Williams, K.C.B., K.T.S., died 1832.

few days later a detachment of the Anglo-Portuguese Army (including four companies of the 60th), under Marshal Beresford,[8] which was covering the Spanish fortress, Badajos, repulsed a most determined attack at Albuhera, (May 16th), an action in which British courage and tenacity had never been surpassed. Captain Galiffe, of the 60th, and one Rifleman were present both at Fuentes d'Onor and Albuhera. It is believed that no other individual officer or man in the whole army fought in the two battles.

In October some Rifle companies were present at the surprise of the French at Arroyo des Molinos, where Captain Blassière distinguished himself by penetrating into the town on the previous night.

The next year, 1812, opened with the siege, assault, and capture of Ciudad Rodrigo, and Badajos, fortresses on the Spanish frontier. Sending *Hill* to destroy the bridge of Almarez, and advancing into Spain, *Wellington* on the 22nd of July defeated Marmont at the decisive Battle of Salamanca, (July 22nd). The English general thereupon marched towards Madrid, and, driving before him the King, Joseph Buonaparte, entered the capital in triumph on the 12th of August. But the French were so strongly reinforced that the British troops were obliged to retire for the winter to Portugal.

In May, 1813, the Army finally quitted Portugal, and again advancing drove the French northwards by brilliant strategy. On the 21st of June *Wellington* gained a splendid victory over King Joseph at Vittoria, capturing 150 guns and his whole transport. The 3rd Division, containing the Headquarter companies of the Regiment, played an especially brilliant part by a diagonal attack upon the enemy's position at a critical moment. Ignominiously driven from Spain the French Army rallied on the frontier river Bidassoa, where Soult assumed command, having been despatched by Napoleon to supersede his brother King Joseph and Marshal Jourdan.

He immediately attacked the English, but was defeated with great slaughter at the Battle of the Pyrenees, which lasted eight days, July the 24th to August the 2nd. The 5th Battalion was at this time commanded by Lieut.-Colonel Fitzgerald.[9] *Wellington*, then advancing into France, forced the passage of the Bidassoa on October the 7th, and carried the strongly fortified lines of the French upon the Nivelle

---

8. Afterwards General Viscount Beresford, G.C.B., G.C.H., Colonel-in-Chief of the 60th Rifles, 1852-54.

9. Afterward Field-Marshal Sir John Foster Fitzgerald, G.C.B. Born 178C, died 1877, aged 91.

River, after a battle which he considered, the finest action of his career. The campaign ended in a further victory on the Nive, after a battle lasting five days, (Dec. 9th to 13th).

In February, 1814, occurred one of the most brilliant manoeuvres of the war—the famous passage of the Adour, which was forced in the teeth of a division of the French Army, the company of the 60th leading the advance of the Guards' Brigade, to which it was attached. On the 27th of the same month Soult was again totally defeated at Orthes, (Feb. 27th).

Wellington, following up this victory, advanced on Toulouse, where, on the 10th of April, the British troops won the last of the fourteen great battles fought in the Peninsular War, (April 15th), in twelve of which the Regiment had taken a glorious part. The repulse of a sortie from Bayonne was the final episode of this memorable war, which was terminated by the abdication of the Emperor Napoleon.

Thus closes a momentous record of gallant achievements of the Regiment. Among the officers of the 5th Battalion who distinguished themselves during the Peninsular War, besides those already mentioned, were Major Woodgate,[10] Lieut.-Colonel Galiffe,[11] Captain Schoedde,[12] and Captain Blassière.

Major-Generals Sir Henry Clinton, Sir George Murray, and Sir James Kempt, Colonels Commandant of the Regiment, also served with distinction.

To continue the history of the other battalions of the Regiment at this period, the 2nd Battalion, in January, 1809, after Corunna, had returned to the Channel Islands, and thence to the West Indies. The 1st Battalion, which had previously always been quartered in America, was in 1810, together with the 4th Battalion, brought to England, whence it shortly afterwards proceeded to the Cape of Good Hope, and the 4th Battalion was sent to Dominica.

A 7th and 8th Battalion were added in 1813, the former raised at Gibraltar and the latter at Lisbon. Both battalions were dressed in green, which colour at the end of 1815 was adopted for the whole Regiment.

At the conclusion of the war with France the Regiment was reduced to two battalions, of which the 1st was called "The Rifle" Battalion and the 2nd "The Light Infantry" Battalion. In 1824 the 2nd

---

10. Afterwards colonel and C.B., died 1861. 11. Afterwards colonel and C.B., died 1848. 12. Afterwards Lieut.-General Sir James Holmes Schoedde, K.C.B., who received thirteen clasps with his war medal. Born 1786, died 1861.

Battalion became also a Rifle Battalion, and the Regiment dropping its old title of "Royal Americans" was granted by George IV the name of "The Duke of York's Own Rifle Corps," dated June 4th.

4

1825-1856.—Sikh War.—
South Africa

In 1827 took place the death of Field-Marshal H.R.H. the Duke of York,[1] who had been Colonel-in-Chief for thirty years, and had given his name to the Regiment. He was succeeded by his brother, Field-Marshal H.R.H. Adolphus, Duke of Cambridge.[2] In 1830 the title of the Regiment, by order of William IV, was again changed to The King's Royal Rifle Corps.

A long peace followed the great wars of the Napoleonic period, and from Toulouse in 1814 until the Sikh War in 1848 the Regiment was not engaged on active service. But from 1848 onwards the British Army entered upon a famous series of campaigns, in nearly all of which the Regiment has taken a memorable share. Its success may be said to be largely due to the excellence and the example of the 1st Battalion, which—directly inheriting the Peninsular honours and traditions of the 5th Battalion as Riflemen—had maintained, in spite of the long peace, its reputation for smartness, discipline, and general efficiency for War.

Fortunate at this period in many officers of great experience, the Regiment owed much to Lieut.-Colonel the Hon. Henry Richard Molyneux,[3] who commanded the 1st Battalion (then quartered in the Mediterranean) from 1836 until his untimely death in 1841. The high efficiency of the battalion and its strong *esprit de corps* when it sailed

---

1. His Royal Highness's sword and belts were presented to the officers of the 1st Battalion by H.M. King George IV, and are now in the Officers' Mess.
2. The seventh son of George III and the Father of the late Field-Marshal H.R.H. George Duke of Cambridge, Colonel-in-Chief, 1869-1904.
3. 3rd son of 2nd Earl of Sefton. Born 27th August, 1800; died 1841.

for India in 1845, under his successor Lieut.-Colonel the Hon. Henry Dundas,[4] were largely due to his strong personality and to his powers of organisation. Dundas commanded the battalion from 1845 to 1854 with conspicuous success. In the Sikh War, both as colonel and as brigadier-general, he showed the highest qualities of leadership and courage, and throughout the nine years of his command the battalion held a foremost place in the British Army in India.

It was thus under these favourable circumstances that the Regiment began its career in the East, (1848-49, Punjaub), and under Dundas played a prominent part in the Sikh War. Employed in covering the advance, it was foremost in the storming of the city of Mooltan, (Jan. 22nd, 1849). "Nothing could exceed the gallantry and discipline of the 60th Royal Rifles" are the words of the *Gazette*, 7th of March, 1849.

Subsequently, by forced marches, the Battalion joined the army under Lord Gough[5] in time to share in the final Battle of Goojerat, (Feb. 21st, 1849), a victory over a combined force of 60,000 Sikhs and Afghans. The result of this triumph of British arms was the annexation of the Punjaub, and the retreat of the Ameer Dost Mahomed Khan with the Afghan army beyond the Khyber Pass.

Upon the 8th of July, 1850, H.R.H. Adolphus Duke of Cambridge died, and was succeeded as Colonel-in-Chief by Field-Marshal H.R.H. Prince Albert, Consort of Her late Majesty Queen Victoria.

In 1851 the 2nd Battalion, which had been on home service since 1847, embarked for South Africa, and was employed in the Kaffir War during that and the two following years. It took part under Lieut.-Colonel Nesbitt in many actions with the enemy, including the passage of the Great Kei, the attack on the Iron Mountain (March 10th, 1852), and the operations for clearing the Water Kloof (May 17th, 1852).

A detachment of the 2nd Battalion (forty-one all ranks, with seven

---

4. Afterwards General Viscount Melville, G.C.B.. Colonel Commandant 1864- 1875. Born in 1800, entered Coldstream Guards 1819; purchased unattached majority 1826; M.P. 1826-29; purchased Lieut.-Colonelcy 83rd Regiment, which he commanded for fifteen years; assisted in suppression of the Papineau Rebellion in Canada; C.B. In July, 1844, exchanged to command 1st Battalion 60th Rifles, and took it to India 1845, until promoted Major-General 1854. Served with great distinction in the Punjaub Campaign, 1848-49, both at Mooltan and Goojerat. Succeeded his father as 3rd Viscount 1851.
5. Afterwards Field-Marshal Viscount Gough, K.P., G.C.B., Colonel-in-Chief 1854-1869.

women and thirteen children) formed a portion of the troops on board the ill-fated troopship *Birkenhead*, which, on the night of February the 26th, 1852, was wrecked on the South African coast under conditions which evoked from the troops on board a memorable display of steady discipline and serene courage in the face of danger. The men fell in and stood calmly on parade awaiting death while the ship was sinking "without a cry or murmur among them." The whole ship's company with few exceptions perished.

On September the 23rd, 1852, General Viscount Beresford became Colonel-in-Chief, *vice* H.R.H. Prince Albert, and was upon his death on the 28th of January, 1854, succeeded by Field-Marshal Viscount Gough.

In 1855 and 1857 the 3rd and 4th Battalions were raised at Dublin and at Winchester respectively. Thus in 1857 the Regiment again consisted of four battalions.

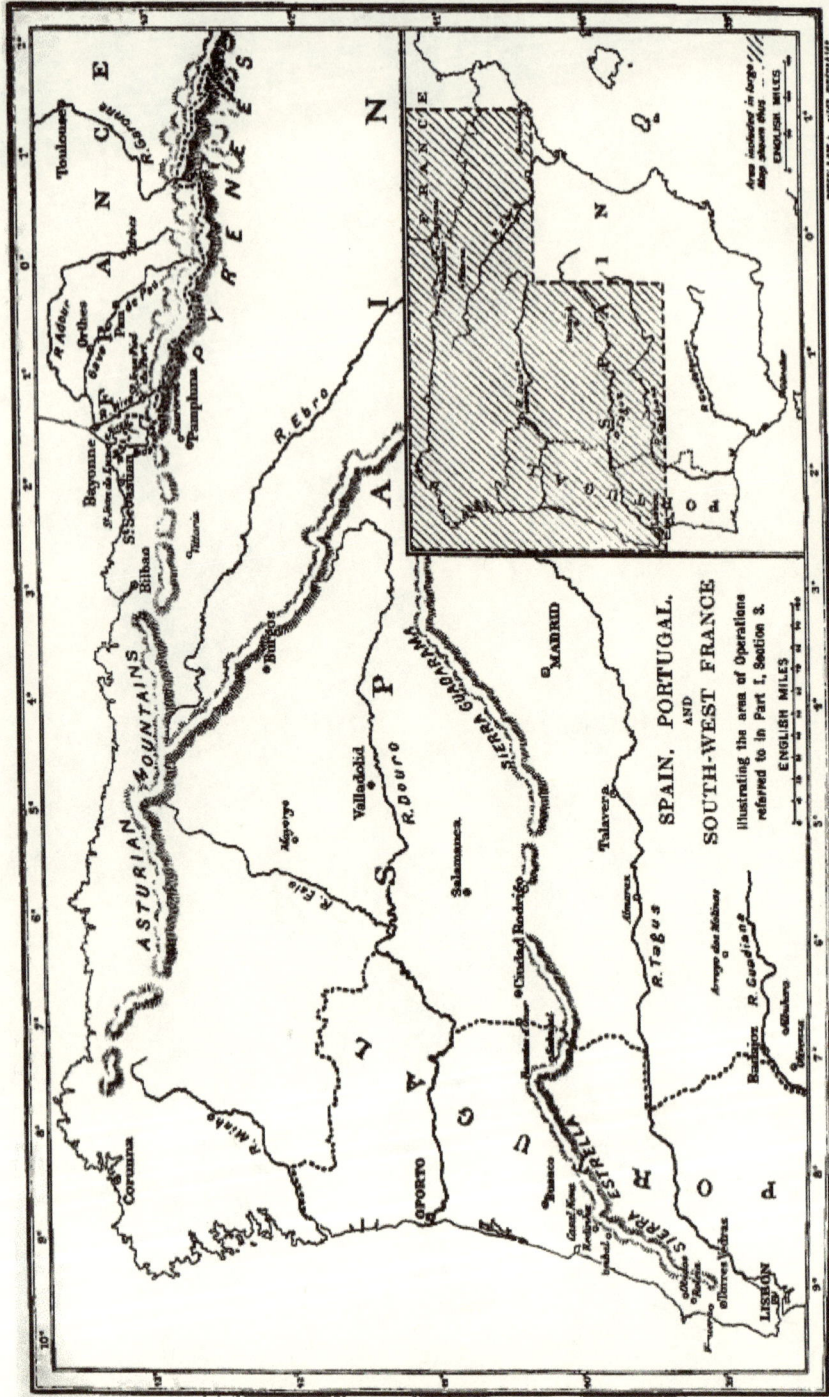

MAP 2 SPAIN, PORTUGAL AND SOUTH WESTERN FRANCE

5

1857-1860.—Delhi, Rohilkund, Pekin

The outbreak of the Great Mutiny of the Native Army in India began on the 10th of May, 1857, at Meerut, where the 1st Battalion was at that time quartered under the command of Lieut.-Colonel John Jones.[1] The battalion at the moment was mustering for evening church parade. On hearing the news it immediately fell in, and Captain Muter,[2] the senior officer present, with great promptitude instantly despatched a company to secure the Treasury. The battalion thereupon marched towards the city, when being joined by the 6th Carabiniers and a battery of Horse Artillery (all the European troops available), it proceeded to occupy the lines of the Native troops, thus effectually preventing the mutineers from establishing themselves in the city, so that they were forced forthwith to retreat towards Delhi.

The story is told that while hurrying to the native lines the battalion came upon the body of a lady lying dead and mutilated by the roadside. This lady was well known both to the officers and men for her devotion and care for the women and children of the battalion, and the men as they passed—exasperated at the sight—raised their rifles in the air and swore to avenge her death. It is not too much to say

---

1. Afterwards Lieutenant-General Sir John Jones, K.C.B. A strong and forceful leader. For his remarkable services in the Mutiny he received the thanks of the Governor-General in Council, C.B., promoted Colonel and Brigadier-General and K.C.B. Died, 1878.
2. Colonel Dunbar Douglas Muter, who greatly distinguished himself, obtaining two brevets during the siege and subsequent operations. He was afterwards a Military Knight of Windsor; and died in 1909.

that the battalion, and their leader, known later as "Jones the Avenger," made good their oath.

Marching in pursuit, under *Brigadier Archdale Wilson*, the Meerut troops fought two successful actions upon the Hindun River, (May 30th and 31st, 1857), in which the 1st Battalion took a prominent part, and on the 7th of June it joined the army under *Major-General Sir Henry Barnard* at Alighur.

At one o'clock on the following morning the whole of *Barnard's* force moved against Delhi. On reaching Badlee-ke-Serai it was found that the mutineers were strongly posted in an entrenched position along the ridge from the flagstaff to Hindoo Rao's house, overlooking the cantonments and city, but after a sharp engagement of about three-quarters of an hour the ridge was cleared of the enemy and occupied by our troops.

Thus began the famous siege of Delhi—a period full of glorious memories to all Sixtieth Riflemen. From then on to the final assault on the city (June the 8th to September the 20th) the Battalion was constantly employed either as outposts near Hindoo Rao's house, or with the various columns which were sent forward to drive the mutineers back into the city, when, emboldened by the strength of overwhelming numbers, they made repeated assaults upon our position on the ridge. It is recorded that the Regiment was during this period engaged in twenty-four separate actions.

On the morning of September the 14th, after six days of bombardment, two breaches were considered practicable in the walls of the city, one in the curtain to the right of the Cashmere Gate, the other to the left of the water bastion. The assault was delivered at three points, namely, upon the two breaches and the Cashmere Gate, while a fourth column followed as reserve. The whole of the battalion was split up in skirmishing order to cover the advance of the assaulting columns, and in this appropriate and congenial duty they greatly distinguished themselves.

The assaults were successful, and after an heroic struggle the city was partially occupied by nightfall. But it was not until September the 20th that the place and its defences were completely in the hands of our troops, and then only after continuous and desperate hand to hand fighting in the streets. Nothing could exceed the determined valour of the Regiment, and every Rifleman will remember with justifiable pride and pleasure that, having joined the army before Delhi, its services were officially pronounced to be "pre-eminent in the memorable siege and capture." [3]

All behaved nobly, (writes Lord Canning, the Governor-General of India in his final despatch upon the siege and capture of Delhi-dated November the 9th, 1857), but I may be permitted to allude somewhat to those Corps most constantly engaged from the beginning, the 60th Rifles, the Sirmoor Battalion, [4] and the Guides. Probably not one day throughout the siege passed without a casualty in one of these Corps; placed in the very front of our position, they were ever under fire. Their courage, their high qualifications as skirmishers, their cheerfulness, their steadiness were beyond commendation. Their losses in action show the nature of the service. The Rifles commenced with 440 of all ranks; a few days before the storm they received a reinforcement of nearly 200 men; their total casualties were 389.

We may conclude this page of the Regiment's history by citing the judgement of the general under whom they served, who described the battalion as "a glorious example both in its daring gallantry and its perfect discipline." [5]

In the following year the 1st Battalion formed part of the Roorkee Field Force under Jones, now promoted brigadier-general, which operated against the rebels from the 11th of April until the 24th of May, 1858.

During this short campaign Jones' force swept through the whole Province of Rohilkund from north to south; fought one battle (Nugeenah, 21st of April); defeated the enemy in three actions (Bagawalla, 17th of April, Barreilly, 3rd of May, and Dojura, 5th of May); assaulted and captured one city (Barreilly, 6th of May); and relieved two others (Moradabad, 18th of April, and Shahjehanpore, 11th of May); destroyed two forts (Bunnai, 24th of May, and Mahomdee, 25th of May); and took thirty-seven guns. It was said of the gallant Jones that "he never assaulted a position that he did not take, nor attacked a gun that he did not capture."

The 1st Battalion again took part in operations in Oudh, under

3. Governor-General's despatch, *London Gazette*, May 18th, 1860, upon the departure of the Regiment from India.
4. Now the 2nd King Edward's Own Gurkha Rifles (The Sirmoor Rifles). It is stated of this gallant Regiment that, when asked what reward they would like for their services at Delhi, they begged for and were granted the red facings of the 60th to be added to their Rifle uniform.
5. Despatch, General Sir Archdale Wilson, 22nd September, 1857.

Brigadier Sir Thomas Seaton and *Brigadier Colin Troup*, from the 8th of October until the 31st of December, 1858. Four successful actions were fought with the rebels, namely:—Bunkagaon, 8th of October; Pusgaon, 19th of October; Rissoolpur, 25th of October; and Baragoan, 23rd of November; and the Fort of Mittowlis was also captured on the 10th of November; thence the battalion formed part of a flying column, which cleared the rebels out of the Khyreeghur jungles. A wing of the 2nd Battalion, which had been ordered from the Cape, also took part in the final stages of the operations against the mutineers.

In March, 1860, the 1st Battalion embarked for England, and in a General Order Lord Canning, Governor-General of India, bore further testimony to the services of the battalion in eloquent and unprecedented terms, concluding with the following memorable tribute:—

> It is not more by the valour of its officers and men, conspicuous as that has been on every occasion, than by the discipline and excellent conduct of all ranks during the whole of their service in India, that this Regiment has distinguished itself. The Governor-General tenders to the battalion his warmest acknowledgments for the high example it has set in every respect to the troops with which it has been associated in quarters as well as in the field; and he assures its officers and men that the estimation in which their services are held by the Government of India confirms to the full the respect and admiration with which they are universally regarded. [6]

The splendid services rendered by the Regiment in the period in its history above briefly recorded may perhaps be equalled, but can hardly be surpassed by future generations of Riflemen. The good conduct, sound discipline, and unflinching courage of the 1st Battalion during its service in India (1845-1860) will always be regarded by the Regiment as marking A Golden Age in its history and a landmark in its traditions. On the 28th of February, 1860, the 2nd Battalion, under Lieut.-Colonel Palmer,[7] embarked at Calcutta to join the Franco-British Expedition to China under *General Sir Hope Grant*. Six months later the battalion took a vigorous part in the assault and capture of the Taku Forts on the Peiho River (August the 21st), and thence marched to and occupied Pekin on the 13th of September.

In September, 1861, the battalion returned to England.

---

6. *London Gazette*, May 18th, 1860.

7. Afterwards colonel and C.B.

MAP 3

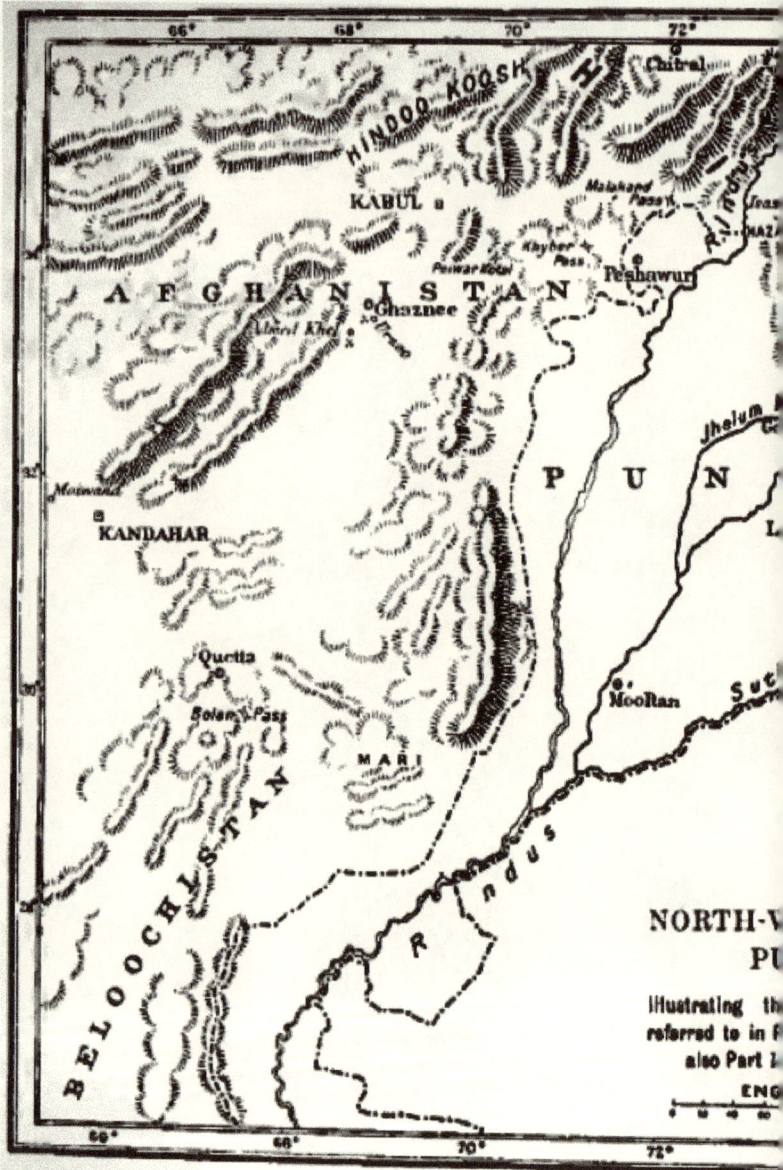

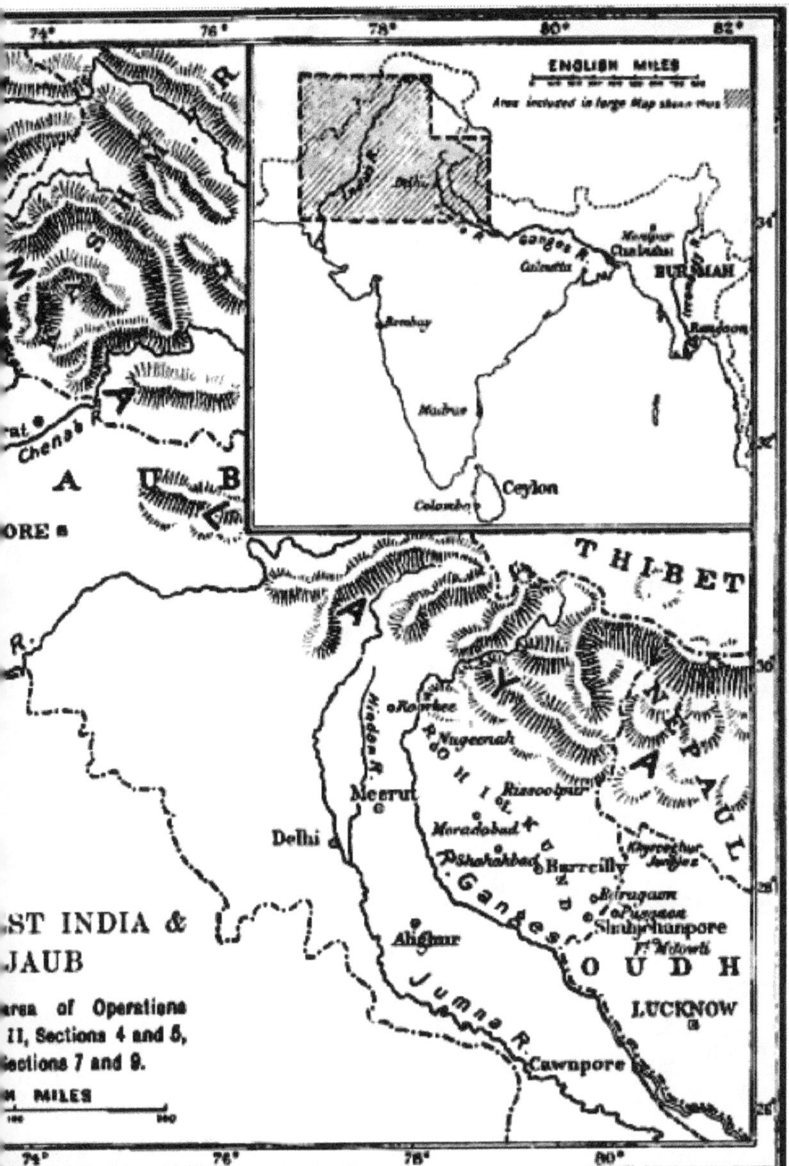

6

1861-1870.—North America, Red River

In 1861 the 4th Battalion was hurriedly despatched to Canada at the time of the Trent affair, when war with the Northern States of America seemed imminent, and Fenian raids were threatened. This battalion—commanded for fourteen years (1860-1873) by Lieut.-Colonel Hawley,[1] an officer of commanding personality and ability—achieved at this period and later the highest reputation for its system of light drill and of organisation then far in advance of the age, a system which has gradually been adopted by the whole Army. The Regiment, both individually and collectively, is deeply indebted to Hawley. Sir Redvers Buller[2] and Lord Grenfell[3] owed their early training to his tuition; and there are few Riflemen of our generation who have achieved distinction who do not directly or indirectly owe their success to his inspiration and teaching, and his influence is still generally acknowledged in the Regiment today. "Hawley, with his pupil Sir Redvers Buller," are, writes the military historian, the Hon.

1. Afterwards Lieut.-General Robert Beaufoy Hawley, C.B., Colonel Commandant, 1890-98: born 18th April, 1821, died 5th August, 1898.—*Vide* Biographical Memoir, by Lieut.-General Sir Edward Hutton, *Regimental Chronicle*, 1909; also *vide* part 4, B.

2. Afterwards General Right Hon. Sir Redvers Buller, P.C, V.C, G.C.B., G.C.M.G., Colonel Commandant, 1895-1908. Born December 7th, 1839, died June 2nd, 1908. His qualities as a distinguished soldier are well summed up by the inscription upon his Memorial Tomb recently erected in Winchester Cathedral, "A Great Leader—Beloved by his Men." *Vide* Biographical Sketch, *Regimental Chronicle*, 1908, p. 157; also *Redvers Buller*, by Lewis Butler.

3. Now Field-Marshal Right Hon. F. W. Lord Grenfell, P.C, G.C.B., G.C.M.G.. Colonel Commandant, 1898. Born April 29th, 1841.—*Vide* part 4, D and "In Memoriam," 16th (The Church Lad's Brigade) Battalion.

John Fortescue, "the great trainers of troops of our own time." [4] *Vide* Section 11, paras, 2 and 4.

In 1869 the 4th Battalion returned to England, and was quartered at Aldershot, where its high state of efficiency was universally acknowledged, and the novelty of its drill and tactics attracted much attention.

Upon the death of Lord Gough, on the 3rd of March, 1869, Field-Marshal H.R.H. George, Duke of Cambridge, the Commander-in-Chief of the British Army, was appointed Colonel-in-Chief.

In 1867 the 1st Battalion, under Lieut.-Colonel Feilden,[5] was moved from the Mediterranean to Canada, and on the outbreak of Riel's Rebellion in 1870 was selected by *Colonel Wolseley*[6] to take part in the Red River Expedition (*vide* map 1). The force, numbering 1200, consisted of two guns, R.A., the 1st Battalion 60th Rifles, and two specially raised battalions of Canadian Militia. After a journey of 600 miles by land and lake, it reached Thunder Bay, on Lake Superior. Leaving Lake Shebandowah, fifty miles east from Lake Superior, on the 16th of July, the Expedition then traversed in boats 600 miles of a region of rivers, lakes, and forest, practically unexplored and trackless, and after six weeks of incessant toil, on the 24th of August reached Fort Garry (now the city of Winnipeg), the headquarters of the rebel forces, under Louis Riel. *Wolseley*, by a brilliant *coup de main*, pushed on with the 1st Battalion in fifty boats, and took Riel and his followers completely by surprise. Hurriedly, the insurgent leader abandoned Fort Garry and the rebellion collapsed.

The direct effect of this achievement, in which the Regiment was fortunate enough to take so prominent and decisive a share, has been the unification of the Dominion of Canada and the opening up to a great and prosperous future of the whole wide region of the great North-West, destined to become one of the most populous and most important portions of the Empire.

Thus for a second time has the 1st Battalion of the Regiment been privileged to play a direct and almost single-handed part in the addition of vast regions to the British Crown in North America: first, in 1758-1764, under Bouquet, in conquering those territories west of the Alleghany Mountains, now some of the most prosperous States of

---

4. *History of the British Army,* Vol. vii, published 1912.

5. Afterwards Lieut. General Feilden, C.M.G., died 1895.

6. Afterwards Field-Marshal Viscount Wolseley, K.P., etc., Commander-in-Chief of the British Army, *vide* chapter 11, D.

the American Union; and, second, in 1870, under *Wolseley*, in crushing a rebellion, the overthrow of which has enabled the prairies of the North-West Territories of Canada to be welded into what are now among the most flourishing Provinces of the Dominion.

PART 3.—1871—1902.

7

1871-1881.—India, Afghan War, South Africa, Zulu War, First Boer War

The overwhelming defeat of the French Armies by the German troops in the momentous war of 1870-71 brought about vast changes in military Europe. A system of compulsory service on the German model was introduced by all the great nations of Europe—Great Britain excepted—and German drill, German style of uniform, and German methods were generally adopted.

In England a strong wave of pro-German feeling swept over the British Army, and military critics advocated the methodical system of the German Army with its stern unbending discipline and exacting method of machine-like *collectivism*, to the destruction of the elasticity and rapidity of movement, with the self-reliance and initiative which makes for *individualism*.

The spirit of the 60th stood out, and did much to counteract this tendency, and to bring about the reaction.

In the autumn of 1878 the 2nd Battalion, commanded in the absence of Lieutenant- Colonel J. J. Collins by Major Cromer Ashburnham, was quartered at Meerut, and formed part of the 1st Brigade, 1st Division, under *Lieutenant-General Sir Donald Stewart*, which, upon the outbreak of the Afghan War, was directed upon Kandahar. *Vide* map 3, North-West India.

After a trying march of 440 miles (one day thirty miles across the desert without a man falling out) Kandahar was occupied without resistance on the 8th of January, 1879.

In the following September there was a rising of the Afghans at Kabul, and the British envoy and his escort were massacred. An advance upon Kabul, the necessary retort to such an outrage, was accordingly made by two columns, and after severe fighting Kabul was occupied by *Lieut.-General Sir Frederick Roberts.*[1] During the winter of 1879-80 the position of affairs at Kabul became very critical, and it was found necessary to reinforce the Army there under the command of *Sir Frederick Roberts.* Accordingly on the 27th of March, 1880, *Sir Donald Stewart's* division of 7520 men was directed to leave Kandahar and march upon Kabul. On the 19th of April the Afghan Army attacked the column on the march at Ahmad Khel, when, concealed in the *khors* and gorges of the hills, a large body of Ghazies charged boldly upon the flank of the first line. Carrying all before them, the issue for a time seemed doubtful, but the stubborn courage of the British column won the day, and the formidable Ghazies, after suffering great loss, were totally defeated. The 2nd Battalion, then commanded by Collins, had the ill-fortune to be taking its turn of rear and flank guard on this particular day, but, on hearing the firing, at once hurried to the scene in time to bear a leading part in retrieving the critical situation, and aid in turning what at one time threatened to be a serious reverse into a decisive victory. G Company, however, under Lieut. Davidson,[2] allotted to the permanent duty of escort to *Sir Donald Stewart,* played a prominent part in meeting the first sudden onslaught of the Ghazies, and did much to stem the rush which at the moment seemed likely to be overwhelming. Continuing the march, the battalion was present at the surrender of Ghuznee, and at the fight of Urzoo on the 23rd of April when the Afghans were again defeated. The column finally reached Kabul on the 28th of the same month, thus accomplishing a notable march. It had covered 320 miles in thirty-five days over a hostile, difficult, and almost unknown country, fought two general actions, and captured a fortress.

In July Ayub Khan defeated a British force at Maiwand, and besieged *General Primrose* in Kandahar. The battalion, already distinguished for its marching powers and steady discipline, was selected to

1. Afterwards Field-Marshal Earl Roberts, K.G.,V.C, etc., Commander-in-Chief of the British Army, whose only son, Lieut. the Hon. Frederick Roberts,V.C, was killed at the Battle of Colenso, December 15th, 1899, when an officer of the Regiment, and serving as A.D.C. to Sir Redvers Buller. Died in France within hearing of the German guns, 1915.
2. Now Colonel Sir Arthur Davidson, K.C.B., K.C.V.O., Equerry to H.M. Queen Alexandra.

form part of the Relief Force of 10,000 men, which left Kabul under *Sir Frederick Roberts* on the 9th of August, and reached Kandahar on the 31st. This march—by the same route as that of *Sir Donald Stewart,* but at the hottest time of the year—was effected in twenty-four days, inclusive of halts, giving an average of 13.3 miles *per diem*, or of 14.5 for the days of actual marching.

On the 21st of August *Sir Frederick Roberts* had notified in Aug. 21st, 1880, the orders of the day that the city of Kandahar was completely invested, characteristically adding that he "hoped Ayub Khan would remain there." This wish was duly realised, for the Afghan leader was found in position for battle, and on the following day, September the 1st, he was attacked in front and flank, and completely routed; the whole of his guns and camp (which had been left standing) were captured by the victorious troops.

On the 8th of September the 2nd Battalion left Kandahar to take part in the Mari Expedition, which lasted for two months and entailed much hard marching; there was not, however, any fighting.

On the termination of the campaign the Commander-in-Chief in India published the following in a General Order:—

The 2nd Battalion 60th Rifles has throughout the war maintained its high reputation for efficiency. In the march from Kandahar to Kabul, at Ahmad Khel, in the memorable march from Kabul to Kandahar, and the subsequent expedition to the Mari country, the 60th Rifles were remarkable for their discipline and marching powers. In the operations above described the Regiment marched 1000 miles in 100 days. No light feat anywhere, but in such a country as Afghanistan it is one well worthy of record in the annals of the British Army.

On the 8th of September Lieut.-Colonel J. J. Collins, who had commanded the Battalion throughout the campaign, succumbed to fever while on his way to India on sick leave.

In addition to the war medal, a special bronze star was given for the march from Kabul to Kandahar. It is worthy of note that khaki was worn, and that this was the first campaign in which the Regiment, since it had become Rifles, had fought in any colour but green.

Special reference must here be made to the 3rd Battalion, whose good fortune led it to take part in no less than four campaigns in six years, and thus to justify a claim to being called "the fighting Battalion." Raised in 1855 in Ireland, this battalion had been moved to

Madras at the close of the Mutiny in 1857, to Burmah in 1862, back to Madras in 1865, and to Aden in 1871, and thence to England in 1872. It had, not unnaturally, suffered much disadvantage from its long exile of fifteen years in the East, unrelieved by the experience of active service. It was, therefore, in a condition especially to profit by the example of Hawley and the 4th Battalion, which had made itself generally felt, and there can be no doubt that it derived at this period an immense benefit in efficiency and interior economy, not only from the influence of Hawley and his system, but also from the traditions and example of the 1st Battalion.

Its new commanding officer, Pemberton,[3] and its second in command. Northey,[4] had both been trained under Hawley, and many of its captains and junior officers, as well as N.CO.'s, had been promoted or transferred from the 1st and 4th Battalions to the 3rd on its return from India. These officers and men brought with them into the battalion the vigorous spirit of the Regiment, its flexible drill and tactics, its ideals of rapidity and elasticity of movement, rendered possible by the most careful attention to detail; its extreme steadiness in close formations; and, above all, that assiduous care for the comfort and well-being of the rank and file, which is its great feature. In consequence, the rapidity and smartness of manoeuvre, the strong self-reliance and individuality of the Riflemen, and the excellent feeling existing between officers and men were conspicuously the attributes of the rejuvenated 3rd Battalion. The battalion, therefore, not only won for itself a great reputation as a fighting unit, but conveyed later the same spirit to the Mounted Infantry, for the inception and success of which its officers and Riflemen were largely responsible.

Having been quartered for several years at Aldershot, where it gained much credit, the battalion was at Colchester in January, 1879, when it received sudden orders to embark for South Africa in consequence of the defeat of *Lord Chelmsford's* troops by Cetewayo, the Zulu King, at the Battle of Insandlwana. It landed at Durban, commanded by Lieut.-Colonel Leigh-Pemberton, and marched direct to the Tugela, where, under *Lord Chelmsford* himself, it formed part of the column to relieve Fort Pierson. Leaving the Tugela on the 25th of March, it took a distinguished part in the Battle of Gingihlovo on the

---

3. Now Major-General Sir Wykeham Leigh-Pemberton, K.C.B., Colonel Commandant, 1906. Born 4th December, 1833.
4. Lieut.-Colonel Francis Vernon Northey, mortally wounded at the Battle of Gingihlovo, Zulu War, April 2nd, 1879.

2nd of April, when the Zulu *impis* with a splendid gallantry charged up to the muzzles of the men's rifles, and severely tried the young soldiers of whom the ranks were largely composed. After a short half hour's hard fighting the Zulu army reluctantly withdrew, leaving an immense number of killed and wounded behind them. The casualties were light, but the battalion sustained a great loss in the death of Major and Brevet Lieut.-Colonel F.V. Northey, who was mortally wounded early in the action.

In June the battalion was engaged in the second advance to Ulundi under *Sir Garnet Wolseley*; and in the subsequent pursuit and capture of Cetewayo, which brought the Zulu War to a close, two companies of the Battalion, under Captain Astley Terry,[5] had a prominent share.

The 3rd Battalion, under Lieut.-Colonel Cromer Ashburnham,[6] remained in Natal, and was quartered at Pietermaritzburg, when in January, 1881, the Boers, under Joubert, invaded Natal. *Major-General Sir George Colley,* the High Commissioner and Commander-in-Chief, having assembled at Newcastle a small force, which included the 3rd Battalion, advanced and attacked the Boers on the 28th in position at Laing's Nek. The battalion in part covered the left flank, and in part formed a reserve to the assaulting column. The attack was repulsed with heavy loss, and the battalion covered the retreat, but did not lose many men.

On the 25th of January, 1881, the 2nd Battalion arrived from India in a state of the highest efficiency after its successful experience in the Afghan War. Landing at Durban, it marched forthwith to join headquarters at Newcastle, where it remained until the armistice in March.

The Boers, as a result of their victory at Laing's Nek, made a desperate effort to sever the communications between *Colley's* force at Mount Prospect, and the advanced base at Newcastle. The general accordingly took prompt steps to avert this catastrophe, and thus it came about that on the 8th of February was fought on the Ingogo Heights an action as glorious as any in the history of the 60th. *Colley*, with two 9-pounder R.A. guns, thirty-eight men of the Mounted Infantry, and five companies of the 3rd Battalion, under Ashburnham, marched

---

5. Now major-general.

6. Now Major-General Sir Cromer Ashburnham, K.C.B., Colonel Commandant, 1907. Born 13th September, 1831. He succeeded Colonel Leigh-Pemberton, and commanded the 3rd Battalion throughout three campaigns, namely, Boer War, 1881; Egypt, 1882; Suakin, 1884; with conspicuous success, and was popularly known among his men as "The Lion of the Ingogo."

early on the 8th from Prospect upon Newcastle, crossed the Ingogo River, and, on ascending the heights beyond, was attacked from all sides shortly before noon.

The British position was a *plateau* covered with short grass, rocks, and boulders; whereas the *kloofs* and slopes occupied by the Boers were also not only strewn with rocks, but overgrown with long grass, which being three and four feet high afforded excellent cover. The troops, though completely surrounded, maintained the fight for nearly seven hours, until at last, in the gloom of approaching night and a heavy thunderstorm, the fire ceased and the enemy sullenly withdrew.

The battalion had lost five out of thirteen officers, and 119 out of 295 other ranks; of I Company only one officer and thirteen men were left, but nowhere had the enemy gained ground. The survivors, without food or water, and with ammunition running short, but with courage and discipline still unshaken, then faced the last ordeal of that long day. Little could be done for the wounded, except to collect and leave them with the chaplain, the doctor, and a few other non-combatants; and then, in drenching rain and darkness, only broken by flashes of lightning, the few remaining horses were hooked into the guns, and the little force moved silently across the veldt to the river, which was in flood, and had to be forded breast high. So slippery was the ground from the rain that the horses could not draw the guns; this for the last few miles was done by the Riflemen. At 8.30 a.m. the following morning Prospect Camp was reached after a peculiarly strenuous test of the courage and endurance of the troops.

Wrote *Sir George Colley* in his despatch:[7]

> The conduct of all ranks throughout this trying day was admirable. The comparatively young soldiers of the 60th Rifles behaved with the steadiness and coolness of veterans. At all times perfectly in hand, they held or changed their ground as directed without hurry or confusion; though under heavy fire, themselves fired steadily, husbanding their ammunition, and at the end of the day, with sadly reduced numbers, formed and moved off the ground with the most perfect steadiness and order; and, finally, after eighteen hours of continuous fatigue, readily and cheerfully attached themselves to the guns, and dragged them up the long hill from the Ingogo, when the horses were unable to do so.

---

7. Despatch, Mount Prospect, February 12th, 1881, para. 20.

On the night of the 26th of February *Sir George Colley* decided to seize Majuba Hill by a night march—a hazardous undertaking which was ably executed. The following day the Boers in three assaulting columns, covered by the rifle fire of their largely superior force, carried the mountain with splendid gallantry, and completely defeated the small British force of 414 soldiers and sailors.

Two companies of the 3rd Battalion, under Captain Holled-Smith,[8] were posted upon the lower spurs of the mountain, and with a third company, sent out later with ammunition, they covered the retreat, but were only slightly engaged.

The brave and accomplished *Colley*—dauntless to the end—died a soldier's death upon the summit of the mountain, and deplorable indeed was the loss in officers and men of the force engaged. A peace—insisted upon by the British Government—brought this unhappy campaign to a close little to the satisfaction of the troops concerned.

---

8. Now Major-General Sir Charles Holled-Sinith, K.C.M.G., C.B.

8

1882-1885. Egypt, Tel-el-Kebir, 1882, El Teb, Tajlu, 1884—Nile Expedition, 1884-85—Mounted Infantry

The 3rd Battalion, under Colonel Ashburnham, had been moved from South Africa to Malta, when the outbreak of hostilities in Egypt caused it to be despatched with the 38th Regiment to Cyprus and Alexandria in July, 1882. (*Vide* Map 4, South Africa).

On the 18th of July, shortly after the bombardment of Alexandria, it landed while the city was still in flames, and formed part of the advanced force under *Major-General Sir Archibald Alison*. A portion of the battalion took part with the Mounted Infantry on the 22nd of July, in the first engagement of the campaign at Mallaha Junction, eight miles from Alexandria, and again in the reconnaissance in force on the 5th August near Ramleh.

On August the 18th, upon the arrival of *Sir Garnet Wolseley*, it embarked for Ismailia, and took part in the actions of Tel-el-Mahuta on the 25th, and Kassassin on the 9th of September, when the enemy, about 13,000 strong, was completely defeated.

The battalion, temporarily commanded by Major Ogilvy,[1] formed part of the 4th Brigade under Colonel Ashburnham, which had been organised for the night march of the 12th-13th September and the assault of the lines of Tel-el-Kebir at daylight. The brigade, forming the support of the Highland Brigade, closed up at the beginning of the battle as day began to dawn, and gave a timely assistance in the assault of the enemy's lines.

The battalion in two lines pressed eagerly forward with its accus-

1. Afterwards colonel and C.B.

tomed dash, and, reinforcing the Highlanders at a most critical moment, entered the Egyptian works at about the centre of the position, where Major Cramer, second in command, was wounded, and had his horse shot under him. After an ebb and flow of strenuous bayonet fighting the enemy gave way on all sides, and, suffering great losses, were broken and dispersed in headlong flight. Two days later Cairo was captured, and the war ended, upon which the battalion formed part of the army of occupation.

In February, 1884, the battalion, under Ashburnham, was ordered to Suakin, where it served in a brigade under that distinguished Rifleman, Major-General Sir Redvers Buller,[2] as part of *General Sir Gerald Graham's* force. On the 29th of February it took part in the defeat of the Dervishes at El Teb, and on the 13th of March it was present at the critical Battle of Tamai. The troops were in two squares, one under *Sir Gerald Graham,* commanding the force, the other under Buller. *Graham's* square was broken, and in the confusion some of its men poured a volley into Buller's, causing one face to run in. Sir Redvers at once rode outside the square, and, with great coolness, rallied his men. By restoring the formation he undoubtedly staved off a terrible disaster, for, had this square been really broken, nothing could have saved the whole force. This action ended the campaign.

The history of the 3rd Battalion at this period would not be complete without reference to the introduction of Mounted Infantry into the British Army. It may be fairly said that the creation of Mounted Infantry, the establishment of a recognised system for its training, and the development of its tactics, was largely the work of Officers and Riflemen of the 60th, and in a very special degree of the 3rd Battalion.

The value of Mounted Infantry under modern conditions of war, was established by the phenomenal success of the relatively small force of Mounted Infantry in Egypt in 1882. This corps, raised and organised by an officer of the 60th,[3] who had raised and commanded Mounted Infantry in South Africa during the previous year, owed much of its success to the officers and men drawn from the 3rd Battalion who had similarly served in the Boer war; its high reputation for individual gallantry and initiative was universally acknowledged, and

2. Afterwards General The Right Honble. Sir Redvers Buller, *vide* chapter 6, footnote 2, also Sec. 11, para, 4.
3. Captain Hutton, later Lieut.-General Sir Edward Hutton, K.C.B.; K.C.M.G., Colonel Commandant, 1908. Born December 6th, 1848.

there was no engagement in the war, from the preliminary skirmishes before Alexandria in July, until the capture, by a *coup de main*, of the citadel of Cairo at midnight of the 14th-15th September, in which the Mounted Infantry did not take a distinguished share.[4]

At Cairo, early in 1884, (Nile Expedition, 1884-1885), the inception and scheme of organisation for the Mounted Camel Regiments was also the work of the same officer of the 60th Rifles. The Mounted Infantry Camel Regiment in particular which rendered such distinguished service with the Desert Column under the late *General Sir Herbert Stewart*, was raised and equipped by the same officer, and was largely composed of officers and men of the 60th. Two out of the four companies were commanded by officers of the 60th (Fetherston-haugh[5] and Berkeley Pigott,[6] both of whom had served with the 3rd Battalion in South Africa), and six out of the sixteen subaltern company officers were also Riflemen.[7]

In June, 1886, a comprehensive scheme for raising and training Mounted Infantry in England was first proposed, before a public audience, by the officer of the 60th already referred to, under the powerful wing of *Lord Wolseley*, and in November following Mounted Infantry were raised and trained upon the principles then laid down under Captain Lewis Butler[8] at Shorncliffe from detachments of the 2nd Battalion and other regiments, under the effective supervision of *Major-General Sir Baker Russell.*[9]

When, in 1887, it was subsequently decided to form a regiment of Mounted Infantry for service with the cavalry division, composed of detachments from nearly all infantry battalions on home service, the command and organisation was given to Major Hutton, of the 60th, and, out of the eight companies composing the original regiment, the 60th and Rifle Brigade found two, or one-fourth of the whole corps. The Mounted Infantry movement therefore may be said to owe its inception, and in a large measure its success, to the officers of the 60th,

4. *Vide* "Cool Courage," an episode of the Egyptian War, 1882—*Regimental Chronicle*, 1909, and Official History. Egyptian Campaign, 1882.

5. Now Major-General R. S. R. Fetherstonhaugh, C.B.

6. Afterwards Colonel Berkeley Pigott, C.B., D.S.O., 21st Lancers. Died 1897.

7. W. Pitcairn Campbell, P. S. Marling, A. Miles, R. L. Bower, and two officers of The Rifle Brigade, namely, W. M.. Sherston and Hon. H. Hardinge.

8. Now Lieut.-Colonel Lewis Butler, *p.s.c*, the author of *The Annals of the Regiment*, *Life of Sir Redvers Buller*, etc.

9. Afterwards General Sir Baker Russell, G.C.B., K.C.M.G., etc., a well-known Cavalry General and leader of men. Died November, 1911.

and to their Riflemen.

The Mounted Infantry system thus begun was largely developed, so that upon the outbreak of the South African War in 1899 there were several thousands of officers and men throughout the infantry of the Army who had been trained as Mounted Infantry. It has been rightly said[10] that the ultimately successful issue of the late campaign was in a great measure due to "the large number of Mounted Infantry officers previously trained, and to the long work of preparation carried on before the war by the Mounted Infantry enthusiasts." If this is so. The King's Royal Rifle Corps may lay a fair claim to a goodly share of such an important result.

---

10. *Times', History of the War,* Vol. II.

9

1886-1898.—Indian Frontier, Chitral, Manipur, Wreck of the "Warren Hastings"

In March, 1891, the 1st Battalion, then recently arrived in India, formed part of the 3rd Brigade, Hazara Field Force, and took part in the operations on the Samana Range, where Colonel Cramer,[1] commanding the battalion, was severely wounded; and the command throughout the remainder of the campaign devolved upon Major the Hon. Keith Tumour.[2] The battalion also took part in the expedition sent into the Sheikham country and Khanki Valley, and in the action at Mastoun. (*Vide* Map 3, North-West India).

During the same period the 4th Battalion, under command of Lieut.-Colonel R. Chalmer,[3] formed part of the successful Manipur Expedition in April, and from December in the same year until May, 1892, was continually employed with various columns in Burma and the Chin Lushai country.

In September, 1892, the 1st Battalion took part in the Isazai Expedition. In March, 1895, it again took the field under Lieut.-Colonel H. B. MacCall,[4] and formed part of the Chitral Relief Force, serving with the leading brigade under Brigadier General A. A. Kinloch.[5] The battalion highly distinguished itself in the Battle of the Malakand on

---

1. Afterwards C.B., and died.
2. Now Lieut.-Colonel the Hon. Keith Turnour-Fetherstonhaugh, of Up Park, Petersfield.
3. Afterwards colonel and C.B. Died, 1911.
4. Now brigadier-general and C.B.
5. Now major-general and C.B.

the 3rd of April, and again in the action at Khar on the following day, thereby adding Chitral, to the honours of the Regiment.

At the end of 1896 the 1st Battalion, under command of Lieut.-Colonel M. C B. Forestier-Walker, left India, and embarked on the Royal Indian Marine Troopship, *Warren Hastings*. Leaving four companies at Cape Town, the headquarters of the battalion and the remaining four companies proceeded to the Mauritius, when, at 2.20 a.m. on the 14th January, 1897, the ship, steaming at full speed on a very dark night, struck upon the rocks off the Island of Reunion and became a total wreck.[6]

The troops on board, in addition to the headquarters and four companies of the Rifles, consisted of four companies of the York and Lancaster Regiment, and a small detachment of the Middlesex Regiment, which, with women and children, numbered in all 995. They:

> . . . . . . at once fell in on the main deck in perfect order until 4 a.m., when the (Naval) commander ordered their disembarkation to commence by rope ladders from the bows. . . . . At 4.20 a.m. the position of the vessel appeared so critical that he at once ordered the disembarkation of the men to cease, and the women, children, and sick to be passed out. This order was promptly carried out; the men clung to the side as they stood (the ship lurching and bumping heavily), and passed out the women and children through the fore port; no man murmuring or moving from his post.[7]

At 4.35 a.m., as the ship was in imminent danger of heeling over and sinking, it became necessary to expedite the landing. Owing to the "remarkable courage and exemplary discipline" displayed, the whole ship's company, except two natives, were safely passed on to the rocks and saved. "Lieut.-Colonel Forestier-Walker,[8] who was in command, was the last soldier to leave the ship."

"The Commander-in-Chief,"[9] ends the Special Army Order of March the 13th, 1897, by declaring that he:

> . . . . . is proud of the behaviour of the troops during this trying time. He regards it as a good example of the advantages of sub-

---

6. *Vide Regimental Chronicle*, 1909.
7. Special Army Order, March 13th, 1897.
8. Promoted colonel for his conduct, and was selected for Staff employment as Chief Staff Officer in Egypt, where he was accidentally killed upon the 31st July, 1902.
9. Field-Marshal Viscount Wolseley.

ordination and strict discipline, for it was by that alone, under God's Providence, that heavy loss of life was prevented.

The Regiment will always cherish the honoured memory of Colonel Forestier-Walker and of their comrades, who were thus given the opportunity of supplying one of the finest examples of high discipline which the annals of the British Army can show.

10

1899-1902.—South Africa, Talana Hill, Defence of Ladysmith, Relief of Ladysmith, Transvaal

Note.—As the following section deals with contemporaneous events and with members of the Regiment still serving, it has been considered advisable to adopt a short record of events by battalions and units, leaving to a future historian the compilation of a complete narrative.

First Battalion.

When, on October the 7th, 1899, war was declared by President Kruger and the Boer Government, the 1st Battalion, under the command of Lieut.-Colonel Robert Henry Gunning, was at Dundee, Natal, with the exception of G Company, which was at Eshowe in Zululand, and there remained until after the following March.

At Talana Hill (20th of October), the first battle of the war, the Battalion greatly distinguished itself in the attack of the Boer position, and took a leading part in the complete defeat of the enemy.[1] Lieut.-Colonel Gunning was killed leading the assault, and out of seventeen officers present, five were killed and eight wounded, together with many N.CO.'s and Riflemen. Major W. Pitcairn Campbell[2] thereupon assumed command.

Then came the retreat to Ladysmith by a forced march under peculiarly trying circumstances, and on the 30th October took place

---

1. *Vide Official History of the War,* Vol. I.
2. Now Lieut.-General Sir William Pitcairn Campbell, K.C.B. *Vide* also footnote 7, chapter 7.

the Battle of Lombard's Kop, which, indecisive in its effect, led to the investment by the Boer Army. The four months Defence of Ladysmith was the result, the chief battle being that of Waggon Hill on January the 6th, 1900.

Up to March, 1900, the battalion lost eight officers and forty-three men killed, eight officers and 180 men wounded, and eighty-one men who died in hospital.

After the Relief of Ladysmith, on the 3rd of March, the Battalion joined the 8th Brigade, 5th Division, and was with Buller's advance into the Transvaal, taking part in the passage of the Biggarsberg in May, the attacks on Botha's Pass and Alleman's Nek (8th and 11th of June), the occupation of Wakkerstroom (17th of June), and of Stand-erton (23rd of June).

In August the battalion assisted in the capture of Amersfoort and Ermelo, and was present at the battle of Belfast (August the 27th), when the armies under *Roberts* and *Buller* first joined hands, taking part in the attack on Bergendal.

It subsequently assisted in the occupation of Lydenburg (6th of September), and at the fighting in the Mauchberg (9th of September), and at Pilgrim's Rest (27th of September). On October the 16th, 1900, the battalion returned to Middelburg, where it was continually engaged in minor operations until July, 1901, when it proceeded to Cape Colony. Here it built the seventy miles of blockhouses between De Aar and Orange River, which it occupied till the end of the war in June, 1902.

SECOND BATTALION.

The 2nd Battalion left India, and landed in Natal in October, 1899, under the command of Lieut.-Colonel G. Grimwood, and proceeded at once to Ladysmith, taking part in the Battles of Rietfontein (Oc-tober the 24th) and Lombard's Kop, in which it fought alongside the 1st Battalion. It served through the Defence of Ladysmith, and greatly distinguished itself in the famous fight on Waggon Hill of January- the 6th.

Up to the 31st of March the Battalion lost five officers (including two attached) and twenty-six men killed in action, seventy-five men wounded, and 107 who died in hospital.

After the relief it was under the command of Major the Hon. E. J. Montagu-Stuart-Wortley,[3] and, with the 1st Battalion, formed part of

---

3. Now major-general, C.B., C.M.G., M.V.O., D.S.O.

the 8th Brigade, 5th Division, until the 1st of August, 1900, when it proceeded to Ceylon in charge of prisoners of war.

THIRD BATTALION.

The 3rd Battalion, under the command of Lieut.-Colonel Robert George Buchanan-Riddell, left England in November, 1899, with the 4th Light Infantry Brigade, under *Major-General the Hon. N. G. Lyttelton*, and landed at Durban on the 30th. It took part in all the battles for the Relief of Ladysmith, namely, Colenso (December the 15th), Spion Kop (January the 24th), Vaal Krantz (5th–7th of February), and the fourteen days continuous fighting from the 13th to the 27th of February, including the actions at Cingolo, Monte Christo, Hlangwane, Hart's Hill, and the final battle of Pieter's Hill, on February the 27th, Majuba Day. The Battalion rightly cherishes with pride the names of Spion Kop, Vaal Krantz, and Hart's Hill.

At Spion Kopt[4] it captured by a bold and vigorous stroke the famous Twin Peaks single-handed, rightly considered one of the most notable feats of the war. The final episodes of the assault are thus described in the carefully reasoned account given by the very competent, but distinctly critical historian of this war:—

> At 5 p.m., under cover of a heavy fire from the left half-battalion and from the Naval guns, the right half fixed bayonets and rushed the eastern peak with a cheer. A few minutes later the left half were in possession of their peak also. Away galloped Burger's guns down the slope of the eastern peak, and the pompom from the slopes of the ridge now exposed to fire from above; down the hill and off the open ridge streamed Burger's commandos and Botha's reinforcements.[5]

The key of the Boer positions was won, and the road to Ladysmith open. Lieut.-Colonel Buchanan-Riddell, who had shown a sound judgement coupled with an unusual measure of moral courage, as well as of physical valour, was killed on the summit at the moment of victory while leading his men, and Major R. Bewicke-Copley[6] thereupon assumed command.

At Vaal Krantz, after being engaged for twenty-four hours, the Battalion highly distinguished itself in repulsing the Boer counter-

4. *Vide Official History of the South African War,* Vol. I, also "The Capture of the Twin Peaks," *Regimental Chronicle,* 1908.
5. *Vide Times' History of the South African War,* Vol. III.
6. Now brigadier-general and C.B.

attack.[7] This incident has been graphically and correctly described as follows:—

> About 3.30 p.m., on the 6th February, the British shells had set fire to the grass some 300-400 yards in front of the wall, (held by a battalion of infantry, and) taking advantage of this a number of Boers crept forward and, suddenly bursting through the smoke, opened a terrific fire upon the advanced line, which under this unexpected attack wavered and gave way. The Boers rushed forward, and for a moment it looked as if they would carry everything before them. But the half-battalion of the 60th in reserve saw and acted instantly. Scarcely waiting for orders, they sprang up, fixed bayonets, and charged with a rousing cheer. The Boers heard the cheer, saw them coming, and turned tail.[8]

At Hart's Hill four companies were prominent in the desperate struggle during the night of the 22nd-23rd of February, delivering two bayonet charges and losing over a third of their number in killed and wounded.[9] Part of the Rifle Reserve Battalion was also engaged in this fight. The battalion lost during this portion of the campaign three officers and forty-six men killed in action, eleven officers and 195 men wounded, while fifty-nine men died in hospital, and eight men were reported missing, and unaccounted for.

It is worthy of remark that the 1st, 2nd, and 3rd Battalions met in the streets of Ladysmith on the 3rd of March, 1900, when Sir Redvers Buller entered the town at the head of his army.

After the relief of Ladysmith, the 3rd Battalion, still part of the Light Infantry Brigade of the 2nd Division, took part in the advance through Northern Natal, in the passage of the Biggarsberg, and in the attacks on Botha Pass and Alleman's Nek, 8th-11th June. It entered Heidelberg at the end of June, 1900, and from that date until the end of October it was engaged 1899—1902. in the neighbourhood of Standerton and Greylingstad protecting the railway. In November, 1900, Lieut.-Colonel Bewicke-Copley was selected for command of a mobile column, which, till November the 19th, included his own 3rd Battalion. The battalion subsequently occupied a line of blockhouses between Machadodorp and Dalmanutha, Eastern Transvaal, till

---

7. *Vide Times' History of the South African War*, Vol. III.

8. *Idem*.

9. *Vide Official History of the South African War*, Vol. I.

the end of the war.

Fourth Battalion.

The 4th Battalion was quartered at Cork during the earlier phases of the war, and was engaged in training and sending out reinforcements, to a large extent of Mounted Infantry. It was not until December, 1901, that the battalion, under the command of Lieut.-Colonel E. W. Herbert,[10] sailed to Africa. Landing at Durban, it proceeded to Harrismith, O.R.C, where it constructed and occupied a line of blockhouses running west, and remained there until the conclusion of peace in June, 1902.

Rifle Reserve Battalion.

The Reserve Battalion, under the command of Major the Hon. E. J. Montagu-Stuart-Wortley,[11] was organised at Pietermaritzburg, and composed of officers and reservists of The King's Royal Rifle Corps and of The Rifle Brigade, who were intended to reinforce the Battalions shut up in Ladysmith. It joined the 11th Brigade at Chieveley, Natal, in January 1900, and took part in the operations of the 18th to the 27th of February, namely, Cingolo, Monte Christo, Hlangwane, Hart's Hill, and the final battle of Pieter's Hill. After the Relief of Ladysmith this improvised battalion was broken up, and the officers and men of the Regiment were distributed between 1st and 2nd Battalions.

Ninth Battalion.

This (North Cork) Militia Battalion of the Regiment, under the command of Lieut.-Colonel William Cooke-Collis,[12] volunteered for active service, and, their services having been accepted, embarked for the seat of war in January, 1900. Landing at Cape Town on February lst,[13] it proceeded at once to Naauwpoort, and took part in the operations round Colesburg. Leaving Naauwpoort in March, the battalion was employed protecting the main line of communication and the reconstruction of the railway through the Free State in rear of *Lord Roberts'* army. It eventually took charge of the line between Vereeniging and Honing Spruit, where it remained for a year. The battalion returned home in August, 1901, and was disembodied.

---

10. Now colonel, C.B.
11. *Vide* footnote 3.
12. Now colonel, C.M.G., and A.D.C. to the king.
13. Two officers died on the voyage out.

THE MOUNTED INFANTRY OF THE KING'S ROYAL RIFLE CORPS.

Note.—The Mounted Infantry raised in the Regiment played a distinct and distinguished part in the campaign, it has therefore been considered advisable to separately record their services by Battalions. The establishment of a Mounted Infantry Company was 5 officers and 142 other ranks, organised into four sections.

A company was raised from the 1st Battalion[14] in South Africa before the war; it fought at Talana Hill (October the 20th, 1899), was in the Defence of Ladysmith, and later with Buller's army until it arrived at Lydenburg in October, 1900. After this it was continually engaged in the Eastern Transvaal, until it joined the 25th Mounted Infantry in October, 1901 (see p. 69). This Company lost twenty-five killed and thirty-three wounded during the war.

A company was raised from the 2nd Battalion upon its arrival in Natal. It formed, with a squadron of Imperial Light Horse and a squadron of Natal Carabiniers, the composite Regiment under *Major Gough*[15] 16th Lancers, and, joining Buller's army on the Tugela, took part in the campaign for the Relief of Ladysmith with *Dundonald's* Mounted Troops. After the relief of this Regiment it was reconstructed and became Gough's M.I., and accompanied Buller's army to Standerton, being subsequently engaged in the Eastern Transvaal, Zululand, and the Orange River Colony until the end of the war. The wastage in personnel was such that only two officers and twenty-nine others of the original company then remained, but the fact that twenty *per cent,* of the original horses, received in October, 1899, were still doing duty, constituted a notable record in horse management.

The 3rd Battalion contributed one section to "The Rifles' Company" of the 1st M.I. (*vide* M.I. of 4th Battalion).

A second section was formed in December, 1899, and, joining *Gough's* M.I., fought with *Dundonald's* mounted troops in the Relief of Ladysmith, and was subsequently at Blood River Poort, where it was severely handled and its commander, Mildmay, was killed. This section, in October, 1901, was united with a third section raised in 1900, and joined the 25th M.I. in October, 1901 (see p. 69), when the strength was raised to a full company.

14. *With the Mounted Infantry in South Africa* by F. M. Crum of the 1st Batt. King's Royal Rifles also published by Leonaur.
15. Now General Sir Hubert de la P. Gough, K.C.B.

The 4th Battalion contributed a section to "The Rifles' Company," under Captain Dewar, which, together with the section of the 3rd Battalion, and the two sections from the 3rd and 4th Battalions Rifle Brigade, formed one of the four companies composing the celebrated 1st M.I., organised and trained at Aldershot under *Lieut.-Colonel E.A. H.Alderson*[16] before the war. 1899-1902.

The "Rifles' Company" was temporarily detached, and, landing at Port Elizabeth in November, 1899, joined the force under *Major-General Sir William Gatacre*, which was defeated at Stormberg on December the 12th, where it was specially mentioned for its gallant conduct in covering the retreat. The company then rejoined the 1st M.I. attached to *French's* Cavalry Division, and was at the Battle of Paardeburg, where Captain Dewar was killed; it was also present at the surrender of Cronje on the 27th of February, Majuba Day, and took part in the battles of Poplar Grove and Driefontein, and the entry into Bloemfontein (10th of March). It was at the surprise of Broadwood's Cavalry Brigade at Sannah's Post (31st of March), where it behaved with conspicuous gallantry, and it was at the relief of Wepener, and in the fighting near Thabanchu.

The 1st M.I. were then allotted to *Alderson's* Brigade with Hutton's[17] Mounted Troops, and took part in *Lord Roberts'* advance upon Pretoria on the 2nd May. This Company, therefore, was present in the actions of Brandfort, Vet River, Sand River, Kroonstadt, the Vaal River (27th of May), the Battle of Doornkop near Johannesburg (28th-29th of May), the actions at Kalkhoevel Defile, Six Mile Spruit (4th of June), and the entry into Pretoria (5th of June). It was similarly engaged at the Battle of Diamond Hill (11th of June); in the fighting south-east of Pretoria and at the action of Rietvlei (July the 16th); in the advance to and operations round Middelburg; in the Battle of Belfast (24th of August, 1900); and in the march east from Dalmanutha, including the assault of the almost impregnable position of Kaapsche Hoop during the night of the 12th-13th of September, 1900.

From this time till the end of the war this company, still a part of the 1st M.I., was continually marching and fighting in the Orange River Colony and Cape Colony, pursuing De Wet, back again in the Transvaal, in countless forays and skirmishes, in the saddle night and day. When peace was declared it was at Vereeniging, whence it

---

16. Afterwards Lieutenant-General Sir Edwin Alderson, K.C.B., etc. commanding The Canadian Army Corps, 1916.

17. *Vide* chapter 8, footnote 3.

marched to Harrismith, and the portion belonging to the Regiment was absorbed into the 25th Rifle Battalion of M.I. The reputation won by this company for fighting valour and for general efficiency was such as to do the highest honour to the. two great Rifle Regiments from which it was raised.

The 4th Battalion also sent out two complete companies from Cork early in 1901, which were employed in the Transvaal, and subsequently joined the 25th M.I. in October of that year (see below).

On October the 18th, 1901, a complete battalion of Mounted Infantry was formed from the Regiment at Harrismith—an unique distinction—and consisted of:—

No. 1 Company 1st Battalion (F. M. Crum).
No. 2　　„　　4th Battalion (J. Hope).
No. 3　　„　　3rd Battalion (W. P. Lynes).
No. 4　　„　　4th Battalion (G. Dalby).

The 25th (The King's Royal Rifle Corps) M.I. battalion was concentrated at Middelburg in the Transvaal, and was placed under the command of Major C. L. E. Robertson-Eustace[18] until January, 1902, when he was succeeded by Major W. S. Kays.[19]

The battalion thus organised was composed of officers and riflemen who had been in the field from the beginning of the war, and were therefore tried and experienced soldiers. It joined *Benson's*[20] column at Middelburg, a column of which it was said that no Dutchman dared sleep within thirty miles of its bivouac. The ceaseless activity and success of *Benson* eventually decided Louis Botha, the Boer commander-in-chief, to make a determined attempt to destroy his force. To achieve this purpose he collected nearly 2000 men, and by a skilful combination of his troops attacked the column while on the march near Bakenlaagte upon the 30th of October. By a rapid charge he overwhelmed the rear guard, captured two guns, killed *Benson*, and surrounded the column, but was eventually beaten off. The 25th M.I. fought with a stubborn courage, and by their sturdy gallantry kept the Boers at bay and gloriously upheld the traditions of the Regiment, losing in the action eleven men killed, five officers and forty-five men wounded.

18. Afterwards D.S.O. This most gallant and promising officer died suddenly at Cairo, October 4th, 1908.
19. Now colonel and brigadier-general.
20. Colonel G. E. Benson, R.A., a leader of much distinction and initiative.

Thus— stoutly fought out on both sides by mounted troops of this especial type—ended a fight which has been described as "unique in the annals of the War."[21] The spirit of the Riflemen will best be understood from the lips of one of the wounded in this gallant fight, who remarked that "they were content if they had done their duty, and felt rewarded if their Regiment thought well of them."

The Mounted Infantry Battalion of the Regiment ended its short but brilliant career by taking part in all the great "drives" in the E. Transvaal and N.E. of the Orange Free State, and was finally at Greylingstad when peace was declared on the 1st June, 1902.

RIFLE DEPOT.

The depot, under the command of Colonel Horatio Mends,[22] was at Gosport throughout the war. A narrative of the work of the Regiment at this strenuous period would not be complete without grateful reference to the splendid service of administration, training, and equipment, so devotedly performed by the Colonel Commandant, his Staff, and the Company officers generally of the Rifle Depot.

The adjutant was five times changed, but the quartermaster, Major Riley,[23] remained constant to his difficult duties throughout the whole of this trying ordeal.

It is stated that 4470 recruits joined the depot, were trained, and passed to the various battalions, while many thousands of reservists were mobilized, equipped, clothed, and drafted for duty.

The work of discharge at the end of the war was not less severe, but there is no record of failure or of breakdown, and the success of the admirable system of administration was universally acknowledged. [24]

The Rifle Depot was moved back to Winchester on the 29th of March, 1903, after nine years of exile at Gosport caused by the rebuilding of the barracks which had been destroyed by fire.

21. *Vide Times' History of the War,* Vol. v; also *Regimental Chronicle,* 1902.
22. Now brigadier-general and C.B.
23. Major T. M. Riley. Died 28th February, 1908. *Vide Regimental Chronicle,* 1907.
24. *Vide Regimental Chronicle,* 1903.

MAP 4

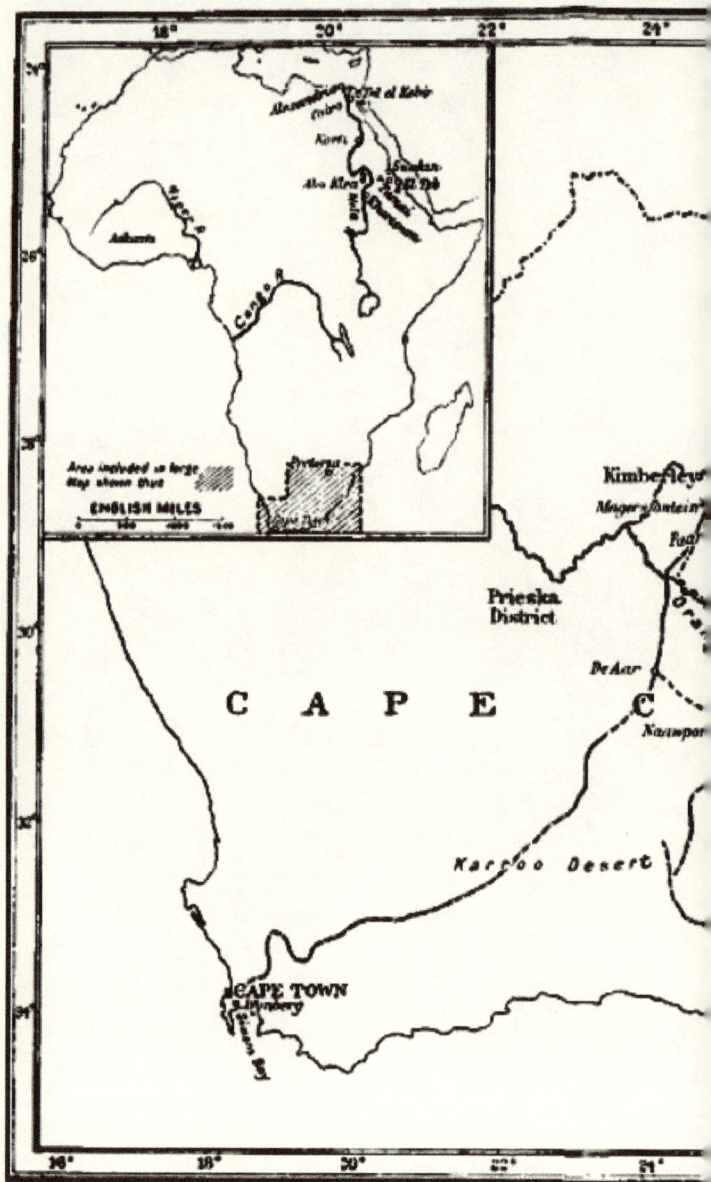

SOUTH AFRICA

Illustrating the area of Operations
referred to in Part III, Sections 7 and 10,
also upon inset map, Part III, Section 8.

ENGLISH MILES

11

1902-1914, The South African War, 1899-1902, Its Objects and its Lessons, Declaration of War, August 4th, 1914

A.

The South African War, which opened on the 7th October, 1899, by the invasion of Natal by the Boers, terminated at the Peace of Vereiniging on the 31st May, 1902. It had lasted two years and nine months: it had cost in money £190,000,000, and in British Soldiers 22,000[1] gallant lives. It had brought into one single arena of war 450,000 men, gathered from all parts of the Empire to serve the Imperial cause and to vindicate the first principles of law, justice, and freedom, as equal rights for all the white races that claim allegiance to the king.

The direct objects of the War were attained, and within five years of its final episodes the Union of South Africa under the British Crown was actually achieved. Far greater Imperial interests were however satisfied even than the Union of Boers and Britons in South Africa. The principles of co-operation in War between all parts of the Empire had been established; the first step towards the great scheme of imperial unity, covering all portions of the King's Dominions—one-fifth of the world's surface—had been tried, had been accepted, and its vast potentialities demonstrated to all who had eyes to see, or ears to hear.

1.

All ranks. Killed and died from wounds or disease	21,940
Invalided from wounds and disease	75,400
Total	97,340

Few realized that this fiery test of the South African War—this Dress Rehearsal—was but the prologue to the far more vast and mighty drama to be enacted twelve years later; the designer, whose prophetic instinct foresaw it all, had died before the curtain fell! With equal foresight and political skill the master-spirit of a consolidated empire had achieved his object, and the life-work of the Right Hon. Joseph Chamberlain was accomplished!

The Regiment had been privileged through its four regular battalions to have a goodly share in accomplishing the great purpose for which the war had been undertaken. If many defects of organisation and administration had been revealed in the army and its system, it had none the less shown the incomparable valour, the adaptability, and the patient determination of the British soldier; as well as the fighting qualities of the British soldier from beyond the seas.

The Regiment lost "killed in action" during the campaign twenty-nine officers and 517 other ranks. Among the former were Lieut.-Colonels R. H. Gunning and R. G. Buchanan-Riddell, commanding the 1st and 2nd Battalions, who fell at the moment of victory while leading their men at the storming of Talana Hill (20th October, 1899) and Twin Peaks (20th January, 1900) respectively.

For us Riflemen the three years of the South African War confirmed the soundness of the system under which we had been born and bred. It remained only to apply afresh and with renewed energy the principles which Bouquet in North America, 1756-1765, De Rottenburg and Sir John Moore in Europe, 1797-1808, and Hawley in later years at home had laid down for us.[2]

B.

In view of the immense increase of Battalions and of Riflemen 1869-1873 which has rendered this new edition necessary, it is imperative that the principles of the Hawley's system (so-called), upon which the Regiment is organised, trained, and administered, should be recognised now and by future generations of our Riflemen. From Alexander and Hannibal to the successful generals of our own day the principles underlying sound military training are the same, but it is upon their thorough and practical application that military success depends. They may be summed up under three headings:—

First.—Assiduous care in the organisation, the training, the

---

2. *Vide* chapters 1, 2 and 5 respectively.

well-being, and the discipline of all ranks.

Second.—The physical and mental culture of officers and men.

Third.—The forgetfulness of self and of self-interest: that guiding principle which prompts us Britons under all conceivable circumstances to "*Play the Game.*"

As regards the first:—

The essence of our organisation and training has always been the development to the utmost of individuality among our officers and our Riflemen. It has been generally recognized in our Regiment that the chief characteristic of our race—the true source of our greatness as a world-power—is the self-reliance and initiative of the individual free-born Briton, and that pipe-clay and the machine-like methods of German *collectivism* have no true place among British troops. The foundation of a successful military unit—be it a Regiment or an Army—is its organisation and its interior economy. The tactics are based upon organisation, and the strategy even must be largely governed by a sound system of interior economy and its administrative value.

Again, careful and minute attention to the food and well- being of our Riflemen are absolutely vital matters. Begotten of these are contentment and good discipline, which make for that sympathy and mutual confidence between officers and men, which have been conspicuous from the earliest days of the Regiment. When officers lead in a spirit of unselfish care and earnest zeal for their men's well-being, the Riflemen will always follow, and if need be die with their leaders.

With such a discipline—a real true discipline of mutual trust and confidence—the utmost steadiness in the ranks and when acting *collectively* is assured, and equally the greatest rapidity, elasticity, and initiative when acting *individually* and in open formations.

As regards the second:—

Every opportunity is utilized to encourage games and sports and to develop the physical culture of officers and men. Besides the regulation gymnastics and drill, the true spirit of sport of every kind is impressed on all. The Persian adage "*to ride and shoot and tell the truth*" embodies the principles held by the Regiment. It will be seen in the paragraphs which follow how successful the Regiment has been in all these important attributes of Riflemen.

The mental culture also of officers and men has never been upon a higher level than during the period covered by this section of its history. Addresses, lectures, theoretical and practical instructions of all kinds are given by the officers, etc., and every encouragement is given to Riflemen to excel in education and by private study.

As regards the third:—

The splendid services rendered by the Regiment during the early phases of the War are sufficient to show how well the lesson has been learnt of self-sacrifice for others, of *playing the game of life* for the achievement of victory in a noble cause. The three thousand gallant lives laid down in the service of their King and Country are the measure of its success.[3]

C.
(The Great Training Period, 1902-1914)

After the Peace of Vereiniging on 31st May, 1902, the Regiment, with three battalions in South Africa and one in India, was distributed as follows:—

1st Battalion (Colonel Bewicke-Copley, C.B., commanding) held the block-house line De Aar—Orange River, Cape Colony, whence it proceeded to and reached Malta on the 17th October, 1902, to be welcomed by the Governor, its Colonel Commandant, Field-Marshal Lord Grenfell. It there remained until March, 1905, when under Colonel Markham it proceeded to Crete, Cyprus, and Egypt.

2nd Battalion (Colonel Kays, commanding) was at Rawal Pindi where it remained until the end of 1904.

3rd Battalion (Colonel McGrigor, C.B., commanding) held the railway Machadodorp—Dalmanutha, Transvaal, whence it embarked for and reached Cork in March, 1903. There it remained under Colonel Pitcairn Campbell, A.D.C, until March, 1904, when it proceeded to Bermuda again under McGrigor.

4th Battalion (Colonel Herbert, C.B., commanding, succeeded in January, 1903, by Lieut.-Colonel F. A. Fortescue) held Harrismith—Orange Colony, until it proceeded to England, and, reaching Gosport in May, 1904, received a gracious message of

---

3. The number of officers and Riflemen who have laid down their lives on the field of battle from August 6th, 1914, to 30th June, 1916, are:—officers, 147; other ranks, 3071; total, 3218.

welcome from H.R.H. The Prince of Wales. The M.I. Company, under Shakerley[4]—which had been since January, 1903, in Somaliland—rejoined in August, 1904, having done splendid service in that very trying campaign: its gallant conduct at the critical Battle of Jidballi upon the 10th January, 1904, which finally crushed the power of the Mad Mullah, was specially commended in despatches.

It should be mentioned that the 2nd Battalion had made good use of its quiet time in India since August, 1900, to win a name for high efficiency, especially in marksmanship, and to acquire a reputation in sports and athletics.

Upon the 6th November, 1903, a statue was erected at Windsor by public subscription to Captain and Brevet Major H.H. Prince Christian Victor of Schleswig-Holstein, who served for twelve years in the Regiment, and took part in four separate campaigns. An admirable officer and a fine athlete, he was assiduous in his care and sympathy for his men. While A.D.C. to Field-Marshal Earl Roberts (during the South African War) he died of enteric fever at Pretoria on the 29th October, 1900, at the early age of 34, almost his last words being "My duty is to my country." Universally regretted, he will always be remembered by his comrades as an ideal Rifleman.

Full of years and honour, the veteran Field-Marshal H.R.H. George, 3rd Duke of Cambridge, died upon the 17th March, 1904, at the age of 85. For thirty-nine years H.R.H. had been Commander-in-Chief of the British Army, and for nearly thirty-five years Colonel-in-Chief of the 60th Rifles. The Regiment owes much to his kindly sympathy, and unvarying thought for its welfare; his memory will always be held in affectionate and respectful remembrance.

General H. R. H. The Prince of Wales, K. G., etc., now *HIS MAJESTY THE KING,* was appointed to the vacancy on the 1st May, 1904.

The 1st Battalion under Markham,[5] after an interesting experience of a joint occupation with our allies of Crete, also of Cyprus, found itself united again in Egypt during 1906. Always maintaining its great reputation for general efficiency, its officers here achieved a prominent place in the polo world: in 1909, after a year at Khartoum, it left Egypt

---

4. Afterwards Major Shakerley, D.S.O. Killed, Rue de Bois, on May 10th, 1916, while in command of 1st Battalion.

5. Now brigadier-general.

for Gosport, where it received a gracious message of welcome from the Prince of Wales, and began a memorable spell of home service after its long eighteen years of experience abroad.

The 2nd Battalion, under command of Kays,[6] and later under Chaplin,[7] moved from Bareilly to Rawal Pindi, and back to Bareilly; thence to Jubbulpore, where it continued to add to its athletic and sporting successes. It distinguished itself by challenging the Gurkha Rifle Battalions at *khud* (mountain) climbing, an especial class of hill racing for which the Nepaulese are celebrated, and though not actually victorious, achieved a moral success of no small importance. Under Hare,[8] who took over command in 1908, the battalion won a foremost place in India for shooting, athletics, and sport of all kinds.

The Kadir Cap—the Blue Ribbon of the pigsticking world, was won by Lieut. Vernon[9] on "Fireplant" against 116 competitors—being the second time only in thirty-nine years that it had been won by an infantry officer. Rifleman McGuire established a record by winning a twenty mile Marathon race at Jubbulpore in two hours, and several private Riflemen distinguished themselves as fine game shots. Among them Rifleman Atkinson—a well-known boxer—killed seven *sambhur*, one hyena, and twenty black buck in a single season. Excelling at football and at games, the battalion concluded its Indian service in 1909 by winning the Queen Victoria Shooting Cup abroad—the Blue Ribbon of the Army Marksmanship. This notable success it followed up by winning the same coveted prize at home in 1910, 1911, and in 1912, thus gaining the unique distinction of being the winners for four years in succession, which earned the especial approval and congratulations of H.M. The King, the Colonel-in-Chief, upon its announcement on February 24th, 1913.

Arriving in England in 1910 the Battalion, still under Hare, received a gracious message of welcome from the colonel-in-chief, and was stationed at Shorncliffe; thus after nineteen years absence abroad it began a memorable term of service at home.

The 3rd Battalion, still under the command of McGrigor,[10] was

---

6. Now brigadier-general.

7. Killed in action at the head of the 9th Battalion while successfully storming the German trenches at Hooge, July 30th, 1915.

8. Afterwards brigadier-general; seriously wounded at the head of the 86th Brigade while forcing the landing at Sidil Bahr, Gallipoli, at dawn upon the 25th April, 1915; now major-general.

9. Now Lieut.-Colonel Henry Vernon, D.S.O.

10. Now major-general, C.B., C.M.G.

moved early in 1905 from Bermuda to Aldershot, where it well maintained the reputation of the Regiment, and was inspected by the Prince of Wales: in February, 1908, it left under Chaplin for Crete and Malta, and thence to India.

The 4th Battalion, under Fortescue,[11] with the traditions of Hawley and his system, still cherished in the Regimental mind, and in a very marked state of efficiency, was winning its way at Gosport and at Aldershot to a foremost place in the Army at home. Later in 1906 the battalion, under Lieut.-Colonel Oliver Nugent,[12] D.S.C, moved to Colchester, where it gained a similar prominence in sport and games to that which it had already achieved in military efficiency. A high compliment was paid it by H.R.H. The Prince of Wales intimating his wish to make a special inspection of the Battalion, and H.R.H. on the 25th July, 1907, proceeded to Colchester accordingly. The colonel-in-chief was pleased to express his unqualified approval in a most gracious memorandum. In 1908 the Battalion, after establishing an unique record of Football successes during the season, won the Army Cup at Aldershot on the 20th April in the presence of T.R.H. The Prince and Princess of Wales: the coveted prize and medals were personally presented by H.R.H. The Princess.

In June, 1909, among the Birthday Honours appeared the appointment of Lieut.-Colonel Nugent to be A.D.C to the king—an honour for the commanding officer, and a special compliment to the 4th Battalion—which was much appreciated by the Regiment. At the end of December the battalion, still under Nugent, started for India, and arriving at Meerut benefited greatly by receiving 373 seasoned Riflemen from the 2nd Battalion. Thus the battalion—in September, 1910, commanded by Lieut.-Colonel Hon. R. Stuart-Wortley[13]—began a very successful career in India where its reputation had already preceded it.

D.

Upon the 2nd June, 1908, passed away the greatest personality which the Regiment has produced. Born on the 7th December, 1839, General The Right Hon. Sir Redvers Henry Buller, V.C, G.C.B., G.C.M.G., joined the 2nd Battalion in 1858. He took part in the following campaigns:—China War and Capture of Pekin, 1860—Red

---

11. Now brigadier-general, and C.B.
12. Now major-general, C.B., D.S.O.
13. Now major-general, C.B., D.S.O.

River Expedition, 1870—Ashanti War and Capture of Coomassi, 1873-74—Zulu War and Battle of Ulandi, 1879—First Boer War, 1881—Egyptian Campaign and Battle of Tel-el-Kebir, 1882—Suakin Campaign and Battles of El Teb and Tamai, 1884—Nile Expedition and Desert Column, 1884-85—South African War, 1899-1900.

Endowed with an indomitable will, great personal valour and un-flinching moral courage, he possessed the highest sense of honour and of devotion to duty. Coupled with these, an absence of selfish ambi-tion and an intense sympathy for those serving with him, underlying a somewhat rough manner, endeared him to his troops in a remark-able degree, and made him a great power in the Army. In earlier days it won him the title of the 'Chevalier Bayard of South Africa'—*sans peur et sans reproche.*

Writes *Lord Wolseley* in 1903:[14]

My very able friend and valued comrade, Redvers Buller, first and foremost among his contemporaries, whose stern deter-mination of character nothing could ruffle, whose resource in difficulty was not surpassed by anyone I ever knew. . . . . Cool and calm in the face of every danger he inspired general con-fidence.

The Regiment owes much to Sir Redvers Buller for promoting its interests throughout his long career. The most distinguished pupil of General Hawley, he put into effect as adjutant-general the principles which he had imbibed in his early years to the lasting benefit of the British Army, and with characteristic magnanimity never ceased to admit the debt he owed to his old Preceptor.

May future generations never forget that it was to the creative power, and military genius of *Lord Wolseley*, the administrative power, the inflexible will, and the knowledge of handling men and officers possessed by Sir Redvers Buller, and the indomitable energy and driv-ing power of *Sir Evelyn Wood*[15] that the British Army of the late eight-ies and of the nineties owes the deepest debt of gratitude.

It was to this trio of remarkable men that we are indebted today for the reforms, the reorganisation, the preparation for War, the train-ing, the discipline, and the mental and physical culture of officers and

14. *Vide The Story of a Soldier's Life,* Vol. II. Field-Marshal Viscount Wolseley died in March, 1913; generally acknowledged to be the greatest military genius of our age: he has left his impress upon the British Army for all time.
15. Field Marshal Sir Henry Evelyn Wood, V.C, G.C.B., G.C.M.G., *p.s.c. Cavalry at Waterloo* by Sir Evelyn Wood also published by Leonaur.

men, which transformed the conservatism of the Army of the sixties and the seventies into the qualities that produced the Army of 1914, which, laying down its life for the Empire and for the world during the present War, has won imperishable renown.

To future history may be left Buller's place as a great strategist. It is enough for us that the legend upon his memorial in Winchester Cathedral has rightly gauged his place in the hearts of the British Army and of his old Regiment as a "Great Leader—Beloved by his Men."

Many important developments took place at this time in the Regiment which have contributed largely to its cohesion and well-being. The Veterans' Association was instituted by Sir Redvers Buller shortly before his death. The *Celer et Audax* Club for officers was developed under Lord Grenfell from being a Dinner Club into an Institution of great value to the general interests of the Regiment as a whole. The ladies connected with the Regiment formed themselves, at the instance of Mrs. F. A. Fortescue, into a Ladies' Guild with H.M. The Queen as Patroness, and H.R.H. Princess Christian as President, for promoting the well-being of the married families, and for ministering to the comfort and welfare of the Riflemen generally in peace and in war.

At the end of 1911 Lieut.-Colonel Northey succeeded Colonel Oxley in command of the 1st Battalion, and in 1912 Lieut.-Colonel Pearce-Serocold succeeded Colonel Hare with the 2nd Battalion, while Charles Gosling and the Hon. R. Stuart-Wortley (succeeded in 1914 by Hon. C Sackville-West) were in command of the 3rd and 4th Battalions respectively.

In 1915 Lieut.-Colonel Northey[16] was appointed A.D.C to the king, an honour very highly appreciated as a special compliment to the efficiency and great reputation of the 1st Battalion and of its commanding officer.

At the time when war was declared on the 4th August, 1914, the Regiment had the 1st and 2nd Battalions at Aldershot in the 1st and 2nd Infantry Divisions respectively, and the 3rd and 4th Battalions in India. It may be confidently asserted that at no previous period in its history has the Regiment as a whole been in such an excellent condition of sound efficiency, or so well prepared for the stern test of war.

E.

The preceding pages are intended to be a record of the manner in which the Regiment has devoted itself during the twelve years of

16. Now brigadier-general and C.B.

peace to preparing for the great cataclysm of war in which the Empire is now engaged. It will be seen that each battalion has thrown its whole energies into making the best use of its opportunities. The same methods have been adopted by all, varied only by local conditions: and the interior economy of the battalions, the comfort, food, and well-being of the men, their training and their discipline have received the same devoted care and assiduous attention. Never has a better feeling of mutual confidence and regard existed between all ranks. The physical culture of officers and Riflemen has received especial thought, and has met with phenomenal success.

The achievements in shooting and the general standard of efficiency have reached the highest level; and the successes in boxing, football, running, and athletics has never been approached in the history of the Regiment. Officers have distinguished themselves in the polo ground, in the hunting field, and between the flags, and notable successes achieved. At the commencement of the War sixteen officers serving in the Regiment were graduates of the Staff College. At the time of writing the Regiment has thirty-one general officers on the active list, of whom twenty-three are, or have been, serving in the field as such.

The mental training and education of N.C. officers and private Riflemen have attained a standard never before thought possible. It may be justly said that no opportunity has been missed, and the utmost efforts have been made to reach the highest plane of efficiency, to rouse the spirit of the Regiment to a white heat of pride in its past services, and at all costs to live up to its great traditions.

H.M. The King, our Colonel-in-Chief, has endeared himself to all ranks by his consistent and gracious thought for the Regiment upon many occasions in India, at Malta, and at home, both separately to each battalion as well as to the Regiment collectively.

During the last fifteen years four members[17] of the Royal Family—cousins of the king—have served in the Regiment. Two of them have laid down their lives for their country while serving in the field in

---

17. Captain and Brevet Major H. H. Prince Christian Victor of Schleswig-Holstein died at Pretoria during the South African Campaign, October 29th, 1900. *Vide* section C.

Lieut. H. H. Prince Francis of Teck, 1889-1890, transferred to the Royal Dragoons, afterwards major, died March, 1913.

Lieut. H. H. Prince Maurice of Battenberg, K.C.V.O., killed in action while leading his platoon near Zonnebeke in the first battle of Ypres, October 27th, 1914.

Captain H. H. Prince Leopold of Battenberg, G.O.V.O., now on active service.

South Africa and France respectively, and one is still a subaltern upon active service with the 1st Battalion.

The interest of His Majesty and the confidence shown by the royal family in the Regiment are appreciated with loyal gratitude, and it is clearly an additional responsibility to the men now serving to merit the honour thus paid to them.

F.

AFTERWORD TO RIFLEMEN NOW SERVING.

The Riflemen of the four regular battalions have now for the most part passed away, and have joined the "invisible army of heroic souls." There remains with us, however, the imperishable memory of their deeds, and the recollections of their valour and self-sacrifice! To follow worthily in their footsteps, to retain the confidence and approval of the king, and the gratitude of their countrymen, is the weighty privilege of the Riflemen now serving.

A German newspaper has written to reassure its readers that "We must think of the old British Army as a thing apart."[18]

It has been said of the *OLD ARMY* by the ablest military writer and critic of our generation that:

> . . . . . . it was one of the most perfect instruments for War of modern times. . . . Admirable in physique and training, possessed of a body of regimental officers without their equals in the world, as well as non-commissioned officers of exceptional merit. . . . *IT WENT OUT, FOUGHT GLORIOUSLY, AND DIED.*[19]

With that Old Army went our four regular battalions! Their spirit is alive, it exists in their successors in the Regiment today, and that their memory shall remain forever as a cherished record is the object of this *Brief History*.

Not by the power of Commerce, Art, or Pen,
Shall our Great Empire stand; nor has it stood:
But by the noble deeds of noble men.
Heroic lives, and Heroes' outpoured blood.[20]

---

18. *Vossiche Zeitung.*
19. "Lost Legions," by The Military Correspondent of *The Times*, October 31st, 1916.
20. Canon Francis Scott, of Quebec, serving in France as Chaplain Canadian Imperial Force.

12

1914—1915. The Great War

BRIEF RECORDS BY BATTALIONS.

Note.—At the present time to relate the History of the Great War up to date—so far as the Regiment is concerned— is manifestly neither possible nor expedient. But a brief Record of the main events by battalions up to the 31st December, 1915, must obviously be of interest to the Riflemen past and present. Such a Record—selected and concentrated from published documents— is merely an outline of the splendid services performed. The Historian of the Regiment will in due time depict their stirring exploits with the completeness which they deserve.

THE REGULAR BATTALIONS.

1ST BATTALION.

The actual declaration of War dates from 11 p.m., Tuesday, August 4th, 1914; it was only eight days later that at 3.30 a.m., on the 12th August, the 1st Battalion, complete in every detail of personnel and equipment, under Lieut.-Colonel Edward Northey, left Salamanca Barracks, Aldershot, for France. Forming part of the 6th Infantry Brigade (*Davies*)[1] and the 2nd Division (*Murray*), the battalion reached Rouen; thence went by train on the 14th inst. to Henappes, and on the 21st by march route to Givry, near Mons, where on the 23rd they

---

1. The 6th Infantry Brigade consisted of Brigadier-General R. H. Davies, C.B., New Zealand Military Forces, commanding:—
1st Battalion, The King's (Liverpool Regiment).
2nd Battalion, South Staffordshire Regiment.
1st Battalion, Royal Berkshire Regiment.
1st Battalion, The King's Royal Rifle Corps.

for the first time came under fire. The brigade had hardly taken up its position, when the enemy's artillery opened, and on the following morning the Retreat began, (August 24th to September 5th).

On August 25th, the second night of the Retreat, the 6th Brigade halted for the night in Marolles. During the night it was discovered that a German force by means of motor cars had seized the Marolles bridge-head. The alarm was raised, and the battalion falling in acted in support of the 1st Battalion Royal Berkshire Regiment, who were attacking the bridge-head, which, however, they failed to take. The battalion remained in support until dawn, and then, forming a rearguard to the brigade, successfully withdrew from the village without becoming engaged with the enemy. Upon the same night the 4th Guards Brigade was attacked at Landrecies.

On the 1st September the 4th Guards Brigade, at this time rearguard to the 2nd Division, became heavily engaged with the enemy in Villers-Cotteret Wood, and it became necessary for the 6th Brigade to return and support them. The battalion went up with the brigade in close support into the wood, and remained there until the 4th Guards Brigade had passed through them, coming under machine-gun fire and shrapnel. The battalion then executed a skilful retirement in face of a strongly pressed advance by the enemy which resulted in surprisingly few casualties, namely, 1 officer, 12 Riflemen wounded, and 1 missing.

During the whole period from August 24th to September 5th the battalion retreated by forced marches. The heat was unusually severe, and there was none of the excitement of a definite engagement; moreover, they were without any news of the momentous fighting at Le Cateau, where, on the memorable 26th August, *Smith-Dorrien*[2] and the 2nd Army Corps immortalized themselves by inflicting slaughter and disaster upon the German Armies of Von Kluck and Von Bulow fourfold as strong as they.

On Sunday, September 6th, the tide turned, and the long and weary Retreat was converted into an advance, followed by the four-day Battle of the Marne, (September 6th-10th)—the brilliant victory of the Allied Armies.

In the early morning of the 10th, during the advance from the Marne to the Aisne,[3] the battalion—up to then not heavily engaged as a complete unit—was acting as advance guard, and was so fortunate

2. *Smith-Dorrien* by Horace Smith-Dorrien also published by Leonaur.
3. *1914: the Marne and the Aisne* by H. W. Carless-Davis also published by Leonaur.

as to come suddenly upon a German rearguard in position at Haute-vesnes; (September 10th), and thus at last arose the chance so eagerly awaited. The enemy in front, some 1,200 infantry and a battery of artillery were strongly posted. Permission was given to assault, and the Battalion, 1,150 strong, under Northey, with its flanks protected and supported by a battery, seized their opportunity, and upon an 800 yards front attacked with three companies in front line and one in support.

From the very beginning of the action a complete superiority of fire was established by its accuracy and rapidity, and, advancing in extended order by alternate rushes, after a stubborn fight of an hour and a half, a complete victory was achieved. The enemy lost 150 men in killed and wounded, and 450 officers and men surrendered; the balance, about 500, retreating in a demoralised condition, were captured by another column.

Writes Northey:[4]

This fight was an extraordinary proof of the good results of our careful training in fire direction, orders, control, and discipline, coupled with initiative. The losses to the battalion, who in this fight so well lived up to their glorious traditions, were 5 officers wounded, 10 other ranks killed, and 60 wounded—not a great price to pay for the annihilation of a whole enemy's battalion. The co-operation between the Riflemen and the Artillery was splendid. The senior German officer, when asked why they had surrendered as they still had plenty of ammunition, replied that our fire was so accurate that they could neither move, nor could they put up their heads to shoot.

During the next three weeks, (September 11th to October 1st), the advance was continued across the rivers Ourcq and Aisne to Verneuil, with constant fighting, which cost in casualties 27 killed, and 5 officers and 136 other ranks wounded.

The battalion crossed the Aisne on the 14th September, was there split up, and upon the same day became heavily engaged. A and D Companies, under Major Armytage, forming the left flank guard to the 6th Brigade, fought touching the right of the 4th Guards Brigade in the Woods above Soupir, where some very severe fighting took place; while B and C Companies, under Captain Willan, formed the right flank guard, and also had some very severe fighting. All four

---

4. *Regimental Chronicle*, 1915.

companies greatly distinguished themselves.

On the 13th October, proceeding northwards by train *via* Amiens and Boulogne, the battalion reached Ypres, where it went into billets; and on the 21st was moved East into the Ypres salient. Here, from the 22nd onward to the 2nd November, it was involved in the desperate fighting that took place, entitled The First Battle of Ypres. This battle proved to be one of the most critical events of the War up to the present time, and may be said to be, with Smith-Dorrien's battle at Le Cateau on August 26th, the crowning glories of the Old Army. (*Vide* "In Memoriam," First and Second Battle of Ypres.)

From October 22nd to 25th the 1st Battalion was in support N.E. of Ypres, until moving up into the firing line on the 26th it at once became closely engaged.

The following day it formed part of a counter-attack against the enemy south of Zonnebeke—an attack necessitated by the retreat of the French and the loss of their trenches. Driving the enemy ahead of them upon a front of 800 yards, the battalion soon came under a terrific artillery and rifle fire. The losses were heavy in officers as well as men; amongst those who gave their lives for the Empire was Prince Maurice of Battenberg. He fell on the top of the ridge, mortally wounded while gallantly leading his platoon, and died shortly afterwards. Pressing forward, the battalion recovered the trenches lost by the French, and speedily made good their position. Situated at the very point of the notorious salient, the battalion came under a very heavy and continuous bombardment, but gallantly held on until the 31st.

After dark on that day it was withdrawn from this sector for a rest, and sent to Hooge Château on the Ypres-Menin road to support the 1st Division. At midday on the 1st November the battalion reached its destination, and later in the day, at 9 p.m., B, C, and D Companies were moved forward with 200 men of the 1st Coldstream Guards on the left, and three Companies of the 1st Royal Berkshires on the right, under Captain Willan, of the 1st Battalion, to hold a section of the trenches running south from Ypres-Gheluveldt-Menin Road, about 500 yards west of Gheluveldt. Their thin line was subjected to a long bombardment, followed by an advance of the enemy's infantry.

A company, with Battalion Headquarters, was at this time detailed to Reserve elsewhere, and only heard later of the catastrophe to their comrades which followed. The 2nd Battalion had just previously held with admirable tenacity a position at Gheluveldt near this very ground, but had been withdrawn for a rest, and the turn of the 1st Battalion had now come. The attack developed, and was pressed by the enemy with renewed and desperate energy and determination: strongly reinforced, and covered by a curtain of artillery, like a rising tide they advanced with overwhelming and irresistible force. At 11 a.m. it was known that, over-powered by the advancing enemy's masses, the troops on the left had broken, and that those on the right had been similarly forced back by sheer weight; but still the three companies the 1st Battalion held on.

The exact incidents of the fight continued at this juncture, as glorious as they were tragic, by which the battalion lost the greater part of B, C, and D Companies in killed, wounded, and missing, can only be conjectured, as there were no survivors to tell the tale. They may be known at the end of the War. It is only certain that the enemy by a furious onslaught with greatly superior numbers, attacked the salient at Gheluveldt on the Menin Road, and, driving back the neighbouring infantry, had swept forward on either flank unknown to the three companies in front line, and thus had completely isolated and surrounded them. Unaided, the three companies maintained a desperate fight, but were never seen again.

The following list of casualties tells its own tale, and although the battalion was almost immediately made up again to its establishment, the original Battalion as it had left Aldershot on the 12th August had practically ceased to exist:—

Casualties—August 23rd—November. 18th, 1914.[5]

	Killed	Wounded	Missing and unaccounted for	Accidentally shot
Officers	5	23	9	1
Other ranks	90	417	490	2
	Total (exclusive of sick in hospital)			1037

On December 23rd the battalion, already re-formed, was again in the fighting line, and its commanding officer, Colonel Northey, was shortly afterwards promoted to brigadier-general of the 15th Brigade.

January and February of 1915 the battalion spent almost continually in the trenches with short spells in billets.

On March 2nd Major Shakerley, D.S.O., succeeded to the command, and Colonel Northey, A.D.C, to the king, left to take command

5. *Regimental Chronicle*, 1914.

of the 15th Brigade.

On the 10th March the battalion took part in an assault of the enemy's trenches near Givenchy as auxiliary to the main Battle of Neuve Chapelle. The new battalion recently reconstructed, shewing itself worthy of the best traditions of the old, displayed the most desperate gallantry, but was brought to a standstill when it was found that the enemy's wire had been untouched by our artillery and was intact. Nevertheless, two officers, two sergeants, and ten Riflemen, by crawling through and under the entanglement, made a lodgement in the enemy's trenches, and held their position for many hours, until all but three were killed or wounded.

Personally congratulated by the Generals of Division and Army Corps, the battalion was somewhat consoled for their losses, which were:—

	Killed	Wounded	Total
Officers	4	2	
Other ranks	153	94	253

From March 11th to May 8th the battalion was engaged in trench warfare and minor services, with occasional spells of rest in rear of the fighting line.

On the 9th May the 6th Brigade was ordered to support the 1st Division in proximity to Rue des Bois, and, after continued fighting, was ordered on the 15th to the Ferme de Bois. After a heavy artillery bombardment, a carefully planned assault was launched 11.30 p.m. by the 6th and 5th Infantry Brigades and part of the Indian Division. The advance was correctly and silently carried out, and, in spite of stubborn fighting by the enemy and intense machine-gun and rifle fire, the three lines of German trenches were taken before daylight, and the new position consolidated.

The casualties were serious, and included the commanding officer, Major G. C. Shakerley:—

	Killed	Wounded	Missing	Total
Officers	5	8		13
Other ranks	22	184	88	294
		Total		307

On May 19th Major Jelf, D.S.O., took over the command of the Battalion. On May 22nd *General Horne*, commanding 2nd Division, inspected the battalion, and congratulated it upon the excellent service which it had rendered on the night of the 15th-16th.

A period of ordinary trench duty, and spells of rest and training followed.

On the 25th September the battalion was allotted to a brigade under *Lieut.-Colonel Carter,* organised especially for the operations in connection with the Battle of Loos, and attached for the occasion to the 7th Division under *Major-General Sir T. Capper.*

At 4.30 p.m. on the following day the Worcester Regiment, closely supported by A and B Companies of the 1st Battalion, under Captain Denison, made an attack on the quarries west of Citie St. Eloi, on the Hulluch Road, which had been recaptured previously by the enemy from some other brigade. The Riflemen gallantly supported the Worcesters in the attack, and although they failed to actually capture the quarries, the battalion seized and made good two lines of trenches immediately in front of the quarries. Here they came under heavy cross machine-gun fire, rifle fire, and artillery fire, and owing to having to cross about 500 yards of open flat ground the Worcesters lost heavily, but happily our losses were not so serious. The remaining two companies, under Major Armytage commanding, came up later, and the battalion was highly complimented by *General Gough.*

The position thus taken was of vital importance to the general line of battle. Holding these trenches with the greatest tenacity during the succeeding days, the battalion beat off three very heavy and determined bomb attacks made by the Germans, each attack lasting from two to three hours, and being accompanied by artillery fire, machine-gun and rifle fire, and on one occasion by extremely heavy artillery and trench mortar fire. The battalion was seriously hard pressed owing to the scarcity of bombs, which were, moreover, extremely defective, most of them being the ball bombs, which had to be ignited by a match or cigarette.

The 1st Battalion undoubtedly saved a very critical situation, as had they given way the whole line would have been forced to fall back on the old German front line as far as the Vermelles-Hulluch Road, and in all probability beyond it.

The share of the battalion in this hard-fought battle, described by Lord Kitchener as a "substantial success," was of no small value. The battalion rejoined the 2nd Division on the 29th, and from October to December did good service in the trenches, varied by spells of rest and training. Major Armytage succeeded to the command on the 26th September, *vice* Lieut.-Colonel Jelf, appointed brigadier-general, and was in his turn appointed to a brigade on the 14th November.

2ND BATTALION.

For nearly two years the 2nd Battalion, under command of Lieut.-Colonel Eric Pearce-Serocold, had occupied huts at Blackdown, a few miles N.E. of Aldershot, as part of the 2nd Infantry Brigade (Bulfin),[6] 1st Division (Lomax), when the order came for mobilization on the 4th August, 1914. Upon the 12th it embarked at Southampton, and reached Havre at daylight the following morning. The brigade moved forward, and was despatched on the 14th by rail and road to the neighbourhood of Maubeuge, which it reached on the 23rd, and was soon in touch with the enemy. The following day (August 24th), the retreat from Mons began, and, the battalion marching for twelve days, out of which seven were as rear-guard, *via* Marbaix, Wassigny, and Soissons, reached Coulommiers on the 5th September—a long and trying forced march of 180 miles in twelve days without engaging the enemy, and without information as regards the situation.

On the 6th September the direction of march was changed to the East, and the retreat became an advance. On the 8th the battalion got into touch with the enemy's rear-guard, and on the 10th some fighting took place; following the retreating enemy, the battalion crossed the Ourcq, and on the 13th, acting as vanguard to the division, reached the Aisne, near Bourg. With prompt initiative the battalion succeeded in securing the bridges over the river and canal almost intact, and thus enabled the brigade, still covered by the Riflemen, to make good a lodgement on the east bank of the river. At 11.30 p.m. on the same evening the order came to seize the high ground above Troyon. At midnight an officer's patrol of eight Riflemen, under 2nd Lieut. Balfour, was sent on to reconnoitre, and with great boldness crept forward on to the *plateau* and located the enemy.

Upon its return by 2.30 a.m. on the 14th, Colonel Serocold, having skilfully made his dispositions, directed the battalion to advance, preceded by D Company (Cathcart), which, pushing rapidly forward, very shortly afterwards came into close touch with an outpost of the enemy, which they promptly charged, and routed. Quickly supported on either flank by A Company (Jelf) and B Company (Foljambe),

---

6. The 2nd Infantry Brigade (Brigadier-General E. S. Bulfin, O.V.O., C.B.) comprised:—2nd Royal Sussex Regiment, 1st Loyal North Lancashire Regiment, 1st Northamptonshire Regiment, 2nd The King's Royal Rifle Corps. The four battalions having served together for some two years formed a highly-trained and most efficient brigade-unit.

and two hours later by C Company (Warre), the Riflemen, in spite of severe loss, seized the edge of the *plateau* immediately south of the Chemin des Dames. A most important success had thus been gained, and the battalion, further reinforced on either flank, advanced, and, sweeping the enemy from their trenches, rushed two batteries of German guns in action near the Sugar Factory. These, unfortunately, they were unable to carry off, and at nightfall, after a fight lasting all day, the battalion was withdrawn from its exposed position into brigade reserve, and the remaining three battalions of the brigade made good the important lodgement thus gained.

On the 17th the fight assumed a more intense character, and the battalion was again brought up into first line. About 4.30 p.m. a number of Germans came forward, with two officers leading, twenty-five yards in front of their men. The whole party—officers and men—continued to advance with their hands raised above their heads as token of surrender, and with their rifles slung over their shoulders. Lieut. Dimmer, with an officer of another Regiment, went forward to meet them, while some of our Riflemen stood up in their trenches beckoning the Germans to approach. Hearing the click of a rifle bolt, Dimmer called to his companion and dropped at once into the turnips. The treacherous Germans immediately opened fire from their hips, but were speedily disposed of by the Riflemen.

A somewhat similar episode took place shortly afterwards, when a body of some 400 Germans made a like treacherous attempt, and opened fire from the hip on the Northampton men, but were disposed of mainly by Lieut. Purcell, in command of our machine-gun attachment.

The inhuman way in which all efforts to relieve or assist the wounded lying in the open were met by the enemy aroused the utmost resentment and disgust of our Riflemen.

The success of this, the first serious action in which the battalion was engaged, inspired the men with a splendid confidence in themselves and their leaders, but the losses were severe:—

	Killed	Wounded	Total
Officers	9	7	16
Other ranks	—	—	306
Grand total			322

The seizure of the heights above Troyon proved to be of great strategical value, and is described by the commander- in-chief's despatch as "skilful, bold, and decisive"; later in the battle this position became the scene of further desperate fighting. Again, on the 17th, the despatch continuing states that "The King's Royal Rifles wheeled to their left on the extreme flank of our infantry line," so that the enemy's attack in force "was driven back with heavy loss."

On the 22nd *Field-Marshal Sir John French*[7] (the commander-in-chief) himself visited the bivouac of the battalion at Pargnau, on the Aisne, where he personally and without the formality of a parade expressed his thanks to the men—a compliment which was much appreciated by the Riflemen and was well deserved.

The battalion remained on the Aisne until the 16th October, when by rail and road it was moved N.E., and reached Boesinghe, N. of Ypres, on the 20th. Late in the evening of the 21st it Oct. 21st to marched to Hetsas with orders to retake early the next morning some trenches that had been lost. The attack took place at 6 a.m. on the 21st, and was admirably planned. The battalion made a frontal attack, while their comrades of the 1st Northamptonshire attacked the enemy's left flank, and the 1st Loyal North Lancashire the left rear. The result was most successful, and great loss inflicted on the enemy in killed and prisoners, of which D Company alone took 130. Our casualties were not great considering the result attained—36 killed and 60 wounded.

Handing over the trenches thus recovered, the battalion returned to Ypres, and with their brigade were in Polygon Wood on the 28th. At 5 a.m. on the following morning the brigade was moved to Herenthage Castle on the Menin Road, and thence late in the afternoon Serocold, in command of the 1st Loyal North Lancashires and his own battalion, was sent forward to Gheluveldt to reinforce the 3rd Infantry Brigade (*Landon*), who were holding the celebrated Ypres salient. The troops, including the 2nd Battalion, allotted to the front line of this very important point, under Serocold as senior officer, strengthened the position through the 30th as best they could. Before dawn, on the 31st, the enemy delivered a furious assault with overwhelming Oct. 31st. numbers of infantry and guns, which forced the left of the position.

At one point the enemy brought up a field gun within 800 yards of the trenches on our left, determined to demolish them. The enemy were here in very great force, and a prisoner afterwards said that there were twenty-four battalions opposed to our small force. A and B

---

7. *1914* by Sir John French also published by Leonaur.

Companies were now practically surrounded—losses in officers and men very great, and some prisoners, mainly wounded, were taken. One officer with five or six men had literally to hack his way through the enemy, but got back with two of his party unwounded. A most serious situation resulted, and nothing but fine leadership and the sheer fighting power of our men prevented dire disaster. At first nothing seemed able to stop the rush of the enemy, and fierce hand to hand fighting followed; but supported nobly by our guns—one 18-pounder gun was actually brought up and fired point blank at the Germans advancing down the main street—the determination and tenacity of our Riflemen triumphed, and a respite was gained. The force was then slowly and skilfully withdrawn to a less advanced position.

Serocold,[8] who had handled his men with marked success, fell severely wounded, and the losses were great, but the situation was saved.

The 2nd Battalion, now commanded by Philips, held on in their new position, and early upon the next morning, November 1st, the Germans, strongly reinforced, again attacked, but were successfully beaten back. In the evening the highly tried brigade was relieved by the 6th Brigade, including the 1st Battalion. The desperate onslaught of the enemy was renewed on the 2nd, in which the 1st Battalion was heavily engaged, and the 2nd Battalion was again brought into the fight to stem the torrent of the German advance; and so for twelve days the ebb and flow of battle lasted, until on the 12th the Prussian Guard was brought up for a final effort.

Attacking with a splendid valour, and in close order, the Guard was only checked at sixty yards distant from our line mainly by machine-gun fire, and fell back with enormous losses. It was here that Lieut. Dimmer[9] won his V.C. Although wounded in five places, he continued single- handed to serve his gun—all his detachment being killed—until he at last fell senseless beside it. The determined valour of this officer—rightly rewarded as he was—was only typical of the unyielding spirit and unflinching tenacity of our men, who took no heed of numbers nor recked of the critical situation in which they were. (*Vide* "In Memoriam," First, Second, Third, and Fourth Battalions.)

On November 28th *Sir John French* again visited the battalion, as he had done after the Aisne, and congratulated them on their behaviour throughout the campaign. " I wish to thank every man personally," he

---

8. Afterwards promoted brigadier-general.
9. Now Captain J. H. S. Dimmer, V.C.

said, "for all that has been done," adding "how grateful I am to you all." Later in the day H.M. the King, our Colonel-in-Chief, accompanied by the Prince of Wales, walked down the ranks of the battalion, and was heartily cheered by the men: a kind and considerate act of His Majesty, which was deeply appreciated by all.

A trying period of five months, (Nov. 29th, 1914 to May 8th, 1915), followed of alternate spells of to trench warfare, and of rest with training and fatigues. In December a draft of men from Rhodesia joined, and were formed into a platoon, which soon earned for itself great reputation for valour and good shooting.

At the end of the year a battalion section of "Snipers" was formed under Lieut. Rattray, which speedily established a marked superiority over the Germans, a superiority which was generally manifest in whichever section of the line the Battalion was serving. The high standard of the men's shooting, and the assiduous care and interest taken in their training before the War now bore abundant fruit. The Rhodesians—accustomed to big game shooting—particularly excelled in this system of "snipers," and inflicted continual losses upon the enemy.

In the early hours of May 9th, the battalion took part in an May 9th. attack upon the enemy's trenches near Rue des Bois. Many acts of individual gallantry took place, but by 7.30 a.m. the attack failed, and the troops fell back.

Four months of severe trench work followed, (May 10th to Sept. 23rd), with intervals of rest and training. On May 22nd Rifleman Marriner earned the V.C. by crawling through the enemy's barbed wire entanglement, climbing a parapet in a thunderstorm, and throwing bombs into a machine-gun emplacement, which had caused much loss.

On September 12th Lieut.-Colonel Philips, D.S.O., was promoted brigadier-general, and the command devolved upon Lieut.-Colonel G. K. Priaulx.

In the desperate Battle of Loos, (Sept. 24th—29th), the 2nd Infantry Brigade. formed part of the general attack at 6.30 a.m., on September 25th, between Loos itself and Hulluch. Unfortunately in the sector of the enemy's trenches allotted to the 2nd Battalion, the wire entanglement was found to be still intact. Two attempts to force it were made, which, in spite of the great gallantry displayed by all ranks, proved fruitless, and after suffering great loss the battalion had to be withdrawn until the Regiments on the flanks, more fortunate in finding the enemy's entanglements destroyed, had carried the trenches and taken many prisoners.

Casualties, including Lieut.-Colonel Priaulx wounded, were:—

	Killed	Wounded	Gassed	Missing	Total
Officers	6	6	1	—	13
Other ranks	80	322	75	19	496
					509

Major Bircham[10] succeeded to the command. During October the battalion was twice engaged, but was re-fitted, re-equipped, and again made up to full strength by October 31st.

Upon the 10th November General Sir Henry Rawlinson, Commanding 4th Army Corps, inspected the 2nd Infantry Brigade, and made an excellent address, praising the brigade for its work at the battle of Loos on the 25th and 27th September, which gave much satisfaction to the Riflemen and their comrades of the 2nd Infantry Brigade, who had seen so much service together, both before and during the War. After alternate spells of trying work in the trenches and rest in billets, the year 1915 ended with a Christmas spent in pleasant billets at Philosophe.

3RD BATTALION AND 4TH BATTALION.

The 3rd Battalion, under Lieut.-Colonel Charles Gosling, upon receiving its orders for active service, was concentrated at the beginning of October, 1914, at Meerut, and on the 10th entrained for Bombay.

The 4th Battalion was at Gharial, in the Murree Hills, when upon Sunday, October 4th, after some days of anxious suspense, the welcome order arrived. The commanding officer, Lieut.-Colonel the Hon. C J. Sackville-West, had already been selected for the Staff of the Army Corps Commander (*Lieut.-General Sir James Willcocks*), and the vacancy was filled by Major B. F. Widdrington, second in command. On the 7th the battalion—after a kindly farewell from their Divisional General, Sir Gerald Kitson,[11] commanding the Rawal Pindi Division,

---

10. Killed on the 23rd July, 1916, while in command of the battalion at the storming of the German trenches at Pozières on the Somme. Exceptionally gallant and devoid of fear—a fine leader—Colonel Bircham had won the complete confidence of his men. (Twice mentioned in despatches; D.S.O.; Brevet Lieut.-Colonel.)

11. Major-General Sir Gerald Charles Kitson, K.C.V.O., C.B., C.M.G., Quartermaster-General in India, 1909—1912.

a well-known Rifleman—reached Pindi by a forced march, a distance of forty miles, in twenty-three hours; and upon the 9th it entrained for Bombay.

At Muttrah, upon the journey down country, the 3rd and 4th Battalions of the Regiment and the 4th Battalion Rifle Brigade met—a joyous gathering of old friends and brother Riflemen, forming a red-letter day of happy augury; all three battalions were destined to serve in the same Brigade, and to win honour and renown together in the forthcoming campaign. The close association of these three Regular Battalions of the Rifle Brigade and our Regiment, together with the intimate relations existing between the 7th and 8th (Service) Battalions of each Regiment in the 41st Brigade of Rifles, have confirmed the close ties between the two long established Rifle Regiments, and have cemented still more firmly the relationship between them, which has always existed. It is to the obvious advantage of both Regiments that these bonds of comradeship, begun in the Peninsula War of 1808 between the 95th Rifle Regiment (now the Rifle Brigade) and the 5th (Rifles) Battalion 60th Royal Americans (now The King's Royal Rifle Corps) upon the fields of Roleia and Vimiera should always be maintained.

The first to reach Bombay was the 4th Battalion on the 12th, which embarked at once, while the 3rd Battalion, arriving the following day, embarked on the 14th upon the same ship; thus the two battalions found themselves joint occupants of one of the biggest, and, as it turned out, the least satisfactory of the hired transports. Upon the 18th November the vessel reached Plymouth, and the two battalions proceeded at once to Winchester, at which congenial centre—sacred to Riflemen—they were encamped upon a wet and exposed site on Morn Hill.

The two battalions formed part of the 80th Brigade,[12] under *Brigadier-General the Hon. C. G. Fortescue,* C.B., C.M.G. (late Rifle Brigade),

---

12. The 80th Brigade consisted of:—
2nd Bn. King's Shropshire Light Infantry.
3rd ,, The King's Royal Rifle Corps.
4th ,, ,, ,, ,,
4th ,, Rifle Brigade.
Princess Patricia's Canadian Light Infantry. A special reference must be made in regard to the Princess Patricia's Canadian Light Infantry. This Battalion was raised in Canada, and was composed almost entirely of N.C.O.'s and men who had served in the Imperial Army and had settled in Canada. It was practically a Regiment of veterans, and a *corps d'elite.*

which with the 81st and 82nd Brigades formed the 27th Division, under *Major-General Snow,* C.B.[13]

The 3rd and 4th Battalions were composed of seasoned soldiers—the average service of the 4th Battalion men being 6½ years; but officers and men had just passed through the long and trying period of an Indian summer; somewhat exhausted by this, added to a long and tedious voyage under very unfavourable conditions, they were in an especial degree unfitted for exposure to the mire and misery of a cold and wet camp during November and December on the exposed slopes of the Hampshire Downs. Under these unfavourable conditions the mobilisation and equipping of the two battalions were completed. It was most unfortunate, but the trying experiences of these battalions had undoubtedly sapped the vitality of the men—veteran troops though they were—and had rendered them particularly susceptible to frost-bite, trench-feet, and dysentery, from which they suffered when moved to Flanders.

Marching to Southampton on the 20th December they embarked, and reached Havre the following day—thence by train and march route to billets at Blavinghem, where the brigade assembled. On the 5th January, after some days of training and instruction in the novel methods of trench warfare, the two battalions marched and took over trenches from the French at Dickebusch, near St. Eloi, north of Ypres, which they occupied until March 24.th.

Dogged by bad weather, it would be hard to overstate the strain and hardship from which officers and men of both battalions suffered in the first three months—many were temporarily disabled; but the excitement and the glory of a succession of minor engagements kept them going. The cheery confidence of the men, and their inspiring determination to justify the reputation which they had brought with them, and thus to rival the remarkable services of their comrades of the 1st and 2nd Battalions, were an abiding element making for future success which no physical suffering could affect.

At this period and in this section the defences were most imperfect; the trenches were not continuous, and effective communication trenches did not exist. No arrangements had been made for draining off the rain-water, consequently the men were never dry, and the trenches became permanently water-logged. The 4th Battalion was particularly unfortunate, and on one morning, after three days in their

13. Now Lieut.-General Sir Thomas D'O. Snow, K.C.B., K.C.M.G., commanding an Army Corps.

section of trenches deep in mud and water, it had five officers and 500 men temporarily incapacitated from trench feet and unable to walk.

In spite of these adverse conditions, the brigade responded to all the calls made upon it, and the commander-in-chief thus alludes to the division of which these battalions were part:—"They are a magnificent set of men, and have done excellent work in the trenches." (Despatch, 2nd February, 1915.)

The 3rd Battalion was the first to have its chance. The battalion was parading at 5.45 p.m. on the 14th February, when an unexpected order came for it to reinforce another brigade who had lost and failed to retake some of their trenches which the enemy had rushed at sunset. It was pitch dark and raining hard, the ground new and unknown, when the battalion, at 11.45 p.m., joined up with a battalion of the Duke of Cornwall's Light Infantry. A joint assault was planned at 4 a.m., which, with some loss in officers and men, proved successful, and the enemy was routed at the point of the bayonet, with many killed and some prisoners. Finding certain flank trenches were still held by the enemy. Colonel Gosling[15] personally directed an attack by two companies at dawn: they had then orders to carry these trenches at the point of the bayonet. Gosling was wounded in the night, but remained at his post, and the German trenches were captured. During this incident Captain and Adjutant Franks,[16] with Rifleman Shee, greatly distinguished himself by clearing out further trenches, almost single-handed, and capturing twenty prisoners of the 23rd Bavarian Regiment.

For this short but brilliant engagement, which cost heavily in gallant officers and men, the battalion gained great credit. Appreciative messages and congratulations were received from the General of Division, and from the General Commanding the Army Corps.

A fortnight later the 4th Battalion had their opportunity, when a brilliant sortie, (St. Eloi), took place on the night of the 1st-2nd March; in this the battalion, under Major Widdrington, took the leading part, assisted by the 3rd Battalion in support.

The Germans had been gradually approaching our line by means of open saps, until at one point they were only ten yards distant, and the time had arrived to stop this aggressiveness. The 4th Battalion, about 300 strong, was accordingly ordered to attack the whole of a section of new German trenches by entering a trench called No. 21,

---

15. Major Long succeeded to the command of the 3rd Battalion until Lieut.-Colonel Gosling's return on May 5th.

16. *Vide* end of this chapter.

near the scene of the brilliant night attack by the 3rd Battalion on the 14th February.

Being characteristic of trench warfare, the narrative is here given at some length in the words of an officer who took part in it:—[17]

We were to hold the trench when taken, and to 'consolidate our position.' To this end D Company, under Captain Poë, was told off to do the attacking, and was to go right on and out the other end with what was left of the Company, making room for B and C (under Major Bircham and Captain Hunter), who were to hold the trench, and carried shovels and sandbags for that purpose. A Company (under Lieutenant Lawrence) was left in reserve. A party of twelve bomb throwers, under an officer, went with the leading Company. The attack was to be supported by the fire of two brigades R.F.A., and the first gun was to be the signal for the advance. The battalion filed along in the order named into the trench, from which the attack was to be launched.

It was a full moon, although there were luckily a few clouds about. When it was judged that about two platoons would have got into No. 21, the signal was given to the guns to open fire at 12.30. Punctual to the second we saw the first flashes in the distance behind, followed by the welcome scream overhead, and then the flash of the burst beautifully low on the enemy's main parapet. It was known that the enemy had a machine gun trained on the point where we had to leave the trench, and soon we heard the deadly sound of it, followed by a roar of musketry and more machine guns, some of them, we hoped, our own on the Mound, and over all the boom and crack of the field guns and bursting shrapnel.

A man was hit in the leg close to us, and there were sounds of others having been wounded further forward, and the line was moving on very slowly, too slowly for it to be good. Presently Barker[18] came limping back, hit in the foot when trying to get out of the German trench, and he told us that we had progressed about eighty yards down the trench, and were held up by a sort of barrier, but that Poë and Eden were getting the men out of the trench to go round it, and all seemed well.

---

17. *Regimental Chronicle*, 1915.
18. Second Lieut. E. H. Barker, now captain.

There was still a forward movement going on, so we waited till the middle of C Company was level with us, and then went on as fast as the ground would allow across the 100 yards to No. 21 past the line of crouching men, between two dead corporals, who were propped up like sentries marking the entrance, and into the indescribable filth of the trench.

The parapet was very low and very thin, and the trench was full of corpses of every Regiment, and nationality and age, and in a variety of attitudes, some still grasping their rifles with fixed swords projecting from the mud, ready to stick one in the leg as one floundered through the mud. The only way to prevent oneself sinking up to the waist in some places was to step on the corpses. Having recovered our breath here, we rushed across the intervening ten yards into the German trench, and found it so full of men that it was impossible to pass along it. So we got out and crawled along until we found a gap in the wire, and then dropped down into it again. The trench was about five feet deep, well boarded and revetted, and had a strong sandbag parapet, with loop-holes on the ground line.

We walked on until we came to a certain corner, about eighty yards along, and here we found Bircham[19] at the head of his Company and about six of D Company. Thirty yards beyond the corner was the barrier, a sort of fort in the trench, very strong with sandbags and wire, and between it and the corner there was a heap of thirty of our dead and wounded. Anything that showed round the corner got a bullet, and as I stood behind Bircham more than one missed his head by inches, and one went through the shoulder of his coat. It was clearly impossible to do anything here, for almost the whole of D Company had disappeared, and with them, as I feared, Poë, Lagden, and Eden.

No one could advance round the corner in the narrow trench, while anyone who attempted to get out and go round was instantly shot by rifle and machine-gun fire from the enemy's main trench some fifty yards in front. So we decided to go and find if anything could be heard from our own trenches further along to the right, for I still hoped that some of D Company

---

19. Afterwards Lieutenant-Colonel, D.S.O. Several times mentioned in Despatches. Killed July 23rd, 1910. *Vide* 2nd Battalion.

might have gone on beyond the barrier. We went back the way we had come, passing Poole, still disdaining to lie down, and swinging his stick as if nothing in the world was going on. We heard nothing, and so came back again: we settled to go and talk to the general on the telephone, after ordering C Company back under cover.

The brigadier ordered that the 3rd Battalion should take over the piece of captured trench from us, and that we should retire behind the breastwork. So we went back, and found Bircham in the same place, and with him Beaumont.[20] The enemy were throwing bombs, but they could not quite reach us, though later one fell and burst between Bircham and Beaumont, knocking them both down, but doing no serious injury. Bircham also picked up and threw back a live bomb, which afterwards burst among the Germans.

It was now nearly daylight, so we left when the relief was nearly complete, and waited for Bircham and his company in the breastwork: but as he had not come by the time it was quite light, we went back to the cellar in St. Eloi, in which was the 3rd Battalion Headquarters, leaving the remainder of the battalion in the breastwork. Bircham turned up shortly afterwards, with a bullet in him, having been hit as he was leaving No. 21 behind, the last man of his company.

The remainder of the story is as follows. The Germans advanced to the corner and bombed Beaumont's company out of the captured trench, driving them back to No. 21. Here they were, naturally, bombed again, and when Beaumont had been wounded twice by bombs, and got a bullet across the chest and through the arm, and all his men had been killed or wounded, except four, those who could crawl retired to Shelley's Farm. Major B. F. Widdrington,[21] commanding the battalion, was wounded in the course of the action.

[22] Poë, Lagden, and Eden were missing, and there is no doubt that they were killed. Eden was last seen at the head of his platoon at the wire in front of the barrier, and Poë was shot at least twice while attempting to lead his men forward out of the

---

20. Captain Sir George Beaumont, Bart.
21. Now brigadier-general, D.S.O.
22. Captain C. V. L. Poë, Captain R. O. Lagden, and 2nd Lieut. the Hon. W. A. M. Eden.

trench. Sergeant Butler was also killed while cutting the wire, and Company-Sergeant-Major Berridge did good work firing at the barrier outside the parapet by the fatal corner. But it is impossible to mention all the brave deeds done on that morning, and we all recognise that many of the bravest acts are never seen at all, even if the actors survive.

The total losses out of about 300 in action were:—Officers, 3 missing and 2 wounded; other ranks—16 killed, 30 missing, 62 wounded, and it is safe to say that all the missing are dead. All the bomb throwers and their officers were killed, and Major Gardiner, R.E., was killed, and another R.E. officer wounded, as well as several of their men. It appears that most of the survivors of D Company (about twenty-four) branched off to the right after passing the corner, and so made their way back to our line.

The battalion stayed in the breastwork all that day, and was relieved at night, but was sent into the trenches again the following night.—(Extract from *Regimental Chronicle*, 1915.)[23]

As a sequel to the foregoing clear and vivid narrative, the following extract from the Despatch of the C.-in-C. will be read with special interest:—

A very gallant attack was made by the 4th Battalion of The King's Royal Rifle Corps of the 80th Brigade on the enemy's trenches in the early hours of March 2nd. The battalion was led by Major Widdrington, who launched it at 12.30 a.m., covered by an extremely accurate and effective artillery fire, but the attack was brought to a standstill by a very strong barricade in attempting to storm which many casualties were incurred.—
(Despatch, April 5th, 1915.)

The two battalions were in support in the action of St. Eloi, March 11th, and were not heavily engaged. On the 9th April the 80th Brigade were moved south to Ypres, and thence to lines in the Ypres salient. Here a contingent of residents from Fiji joined the 4th Battalion and formed a platoon, which, like the Rhodesians in the 2nd Battalion, rendered gallant service.

On Sunday, the 19th April, the Second Battle of Ypres began. The German Artillery opened the operations by an intense bombardment

23. This description of Trench Warfare is given at some length as an illustration of the new style of defensive war.

with guns of a calibre quite new to modern warfare. On the following day the 80th Brigade was moved to Polygon Wood, five miles
east of Ypres, where a defensive position was taken up. On the 24th
the bombardment was intensified, and was further supplemented by
rifle and machine-gun fire, which, advancing, seemed to be perilously
near the line of communications on the Menin Road. The front of
the brigade was shortened to 1400 yards accordingly, with Princess
Patricia's Canadian Light Infantry on the north, 3rd Battalion in the
centre, and the 4th Battalion on the south nearest the Ypres-Menin
Road. The Brigade Reserve had been moved elsewhere to meet the
onward pressure of the German masses.

On Sunday night, the 3rd May, in consequence of the increasing
pressure in the northern sector of the salient, the 80th Brigade was
silently and skilfully withdrawn to a position nearer to Ypres. On the
5th a further withdrawal was made, and a position was taken up east
of Bellewaarde Lake, still nearer to Ypres, with the Princess Patricia's
Canadian Light Infantry and 4th Battalion in front line, and the 3rd
Battalion in close support. On the 9th inst. the 3rd Battalion relieved
the gallant Canadians, who had been badly knocked about, while the
4th Battalion repulsed an infantry attack. On the 10th, after a terrific
bombardment and a strong covering fire of machine guns and rifle
fire, the enemy infantry essayed another advance, which was easily and
promptly scotched by a well-directed rifle fire. Bellewarde Wood was
now an impenetrable abattis, and the two Rifle Battalions were thus
enabled to lend close and valuable assistance against the concentrated
enemy attack to the south upon the neighbouring troops at Hooge.

The 3rd and 4th Battalions in closest touch worked with great effect, and individual acts of gallantry were very numerous. By 6 p.m.
the bombardment ceased, and the further advance of the enemy was
effectively checked. By midnight the 4th Battalion was withdrawn
and a bare remnant collected; on the following day it was moved to a
temporary bivouac, where the men lay down to sleep for a full night's
rest after twenty-six days in the trenches, during a great part of which
they had been closely engaged. The steadfast valour of the Riflemen
was rewarded by a characteristic message from H.Q. Army Corps:—

The G.O.C. is lost in admiration at the way in which the 3rd
and 4th Battalions have stuck out the pounding which they
have received.

On the 14th the 4th Battalion, sadly reduced, was formed into a composite regiment with the remnant of the Princess Patricia's Canadian Light Infantry, and marched under Majendie[24] again into the trenches until the 17th, when the battalion moved to billets in the rear. On the 18th Major Widdrington rejoined the battalion, and resumed command.

On the night of the 12th-13th May the 3rd Battalion was further subject to an intense bombardment, and was reinforced by the North Somerset Yeomanry, who with splendid gallantry enabled it to again defeat an attempt of the enemy's infantry to advance, although our own artillery were quite unable to support us.

On the night of the 13th the 3rd Battalion at last was able to get rest in a bivouac four miles west of Ypres, after a continuous spell of twenty-five days of active work in the trenches.

The losses during the battle were approximately:—

3rd Battalion—		Total	
Officers	killed, wounded, missing	17	
Others	„ „ „	525	
	Total		——542
4th Battalion, in the three days, May 8th-10th—			
Officers	killed, wounded, missing	15	
Others	„ „ „	478	
	Total		——493

On May 21st the 80th Brigade, to which the two battalions 3rd and 4th belonged, was paraded, and *Field-Marshal Sir John French*, the commander-in-chief, made the following warm-hearted speech:—

I came over to say a few words to you, and to tell you how much I, as Commander-in-Chief of this Army, appreciate the splendid work that you have done during the recent fighting. You have fought the second battle of Ypres, which will rank amongst the most desperate and hardest fights of the War. You may have thought because you were not attacking the enemy that you were not helping to shorten the War. On the contrary, by your splendid endurance and bravery, you have done a great deal to shorten it. In this, the second battle of Ypres, the Germans tried by every means in their power to get possession of the unfortunate town. They concentrated large forces of troops and artillery, and, further than that, they had recourse to that mean and dastardly practice hitherto unheard of in civilised

---

24. Now lieut.-colonel and D.S.O.

warfare, namely, the use of asphyxiating gases.

You have performed the most difficult, arduous task of with-standing a stupendous bombardment by heavy artillery, prob-ably the fiercest artillery fire ever directed against troops, and warded off the enemy's infantry attacks with magnificent brav-ery. By your steadiness and devotion, both the German plans were frustrated. They were unable to get possession of Ypres. Had you failed to repulse his attacks, and made it necessary for more troops to be sent to your assistance, our operations in the south might not have been able to take place, and would cer-tainly not have been as successful as they have been.

Your records have many famous names engraved upon them, but none will be more famous and more well-deserved than that of the Second Battle of Ypres. I want you one and all to understand how thoroughly I realise and appreciate what you have done. I wish to thank you, each officer, non-commissioned officer, and man for the services you have rendered by doing your duty so magnificently, and I am sure that your country will duly appreciate your services.

Message from *Lieut.-General Sir Herbert Plumer*, commanding Sec-ond Army, to O.C. 3rd and 4th Battalions The King's Royal Rifle Corps. Extract from Battalion Orders, dated 17th May, 1915 :—

The Commanding Officer is directed by the G.O.C. Second Army to convey to all ranks of the battalion his admiration of their conduct during the recent fighting. The G.O.C. thor-oughly appreciates the excellent work of the battalion in hold-ing on to their trenches, in spite of the very heavy shelling that incessantly pounded them.

Congratulatory message.

The following message has been received by the G.O.C. 80th In-fantry Brigade, from *Major-General Sir Thomas Snow*, commanding 28th Division:—

Battalion Orders, 18th May, 1915.

The G.O.C. Division wishes me to express his admiration at the way you and your brigade have fought and endured during the past four weeks' operations. Twice the brigade has found itself in a position with its left flank turned, and on both occa-sions there has been no retirement, but the exposed battalions have fought it out on the ground, thereby inflicting enormous losses on the enemy.

The manner in which the officers and men stuck to their trenches in the face of a terrific bombardment is the admiration of all.

The G.O.C. deeply deplores the heavy losses incurred, but units will find comfort in the fact that they have taken part in an episode which will figure in, and rank with any in their Regimental history.

He is proud to have command of a division which includes such a 'Stonewall Brigade' as the 80th have proved themselves to be.

He congratulates you on your brigade, and the brigade on its brigadier.

On the 24th May, after a short spell of rest, the 80th Brigade was directed to conduct a difficult night operation, and make a counter-attack against the enemy established north of the Menin Road, near the Bellewaarde Lake. Another brigade had some ground, and the "Stonewall Brigade" was called upon to try and make it good. The 3rd and 4th Battalions formed up at midnight; it was a still, dark night, the country was intersected with hedges and deep ditches full of water. The Germans were soon found to be in force, holding a line with many machine guns. Unfortunately the other brigade which had been already shaken was placed in front, and this fact led to some confusion. The 80th Brigade, however, moving straight for their objective, maintained its direction, but the fire became very heavy. No reply was made, as our plan of attack had been based on a surprise and a rush upon the enemy with the bayonet. Dawn was beginning to break; all hope of surprise had long since vanished, so that there was no alternative but to withdraw to a tenable position.

The casualties of the two battalions were approximately:—

| 3rd Battalion | 3 officers, | 65 other ranks. |
| 4th   ,, | 7   ,, | 159 ,,   ,, |

On June 2nd the 3rd and 4th Battalions were withdrawn June 2nd. into Reserve with their Brigade, which, with their division, was transferred to the Third Army Corps near Armentieres. In this district they remained on duty in the trenches, but without any hard fighting.

On July 23rd Colonel Gosling, commanding 3rd Battalion, was appointed brigadier-general, and for a short time the command developed upon Major Bircham until Major W. J. Long returned and took over command upon August 5th.

On August 23rd Captain Geoffrey Makins, and on September 22nd Captain and Adjutant J. F. Franks, both of the 3rd Battalion—two of the bravest and most brilliant officers in the Regiment—fell victims to some snipers in the enemy lines, deeply regretted by all their comrades.

The 3rd and 4th Battalions, with the 80th Brigade, were moved to the neighbourhood of Amiens on the 26th October, and with the 27th Division (*Milne*) prepared for transfer to Salonika.

On November 16th the 3rd Battalion embarked at Marseilles, and the 4th Battalion at the same port for the Eastern Mediterranean. They disembarked at Salonika on November 25th, and in clouds of dust marched to Lembet Camp. Pitching their tents, they experienced on the following morning a blizzard, which lasted for three days. On December 12th the Brigade marched by the Seres Road to Balza, where a line of defence was taken up along a ridge of hills ten miles north of Salonika. Here they suffered considerable hardship, as the cold was intense, with occasional blizzards, and there were no tents and little shelter.

The badness of the roads and their impassable character during the winter made any offensive movement of the Bulgarian troops most improbable. The attitude of the Greek troops was the cause, however, of considerable anxiety. Lieut.-Colonel Long, C.M.G., was in command of the 3rd Battalion, and Lieut.-Colonel B. F. Widdrington of the 4th Battalion.

Thus in severest winter weather, and at a time of much suspense and uncertainty, the year 1915 closed for these two battalions.

In Memoriam

1st, 2nd, 3rd and 4th Battalions.

The First Battle of Ypres has, like Albuera, been called "The Soldiers' Battle"; it lasted twenty-two days—October 21st, 1914, to November 12th, and is pronounced to be one of the most remarkable contests of the War. 'In it the British Army opposed numbers which were never more than 150,000 to an enemy whose strength was at least half a million. In the actual salient of Ypres we had three Divisions (1st, 2nd, and 7th Divisions) and some cavalry during the worst part of the fighting to meet five Army Corps.' It was left to a little force of 30,000 to keep the German Army at bay while the other British Corps were being brought up from the Aisne. The men clung on—a thin undaunted line, against which the German first line troops were hurled in vain.

'It is to the eternal honour of our men,' writes an able civilian chronicler of the War,[1] 'that they did not break, and of their leaders that they did not despair. Whole battalions disappeared.' . . . . Like Le Cateau, Ypres was an achievement of a truly British character. It was a triumph of bull-dog courage—a decisive victory—and achieved its purpose. Such was the struggle in which the First and Second Battalions took a glorious share.

The Second Battle of Ypres, lasting twenty-four days (April 19th, 1915, to May 13th), in which the 3rd and 4th Battalions took a similarly glorious share, was in some ways less critical than the First. It was, however, a supreme effort by the Germans to destroy by attrition—by a vastly superior artillery—by a completely organised system of machine-gun fire—by the use of asphyxiating gas—followed up by the onslaught of serried masses of an overwhelming force of infantry, our

---

1. Nelson's *History of the War*, John Buchan, Vol. IV.

inferior numbers and our relatively insufficiently equipped troops.

Despite the enemy's superiority in artillery and in machine guns, our infantry undauntedly held their ground, and repulsing with great slaughter the enemy's infantry onslaught, won a great moral victory. During the worst and most critical part of the fighting three Divisions (4th, 27th, and 28th Divisions) held the Ypres salient with a splendid and unshakable valour. The utmost efforts of a desperate enemy—superior in numbers, and provided with a vastly more powerful artillery—had failed. At the termination of the struggle our troops—our Riflemen in particular, felt instinctively that silent, weary, but unshaken though they be, they were the better men.

This failure of the enemy marks the end of the second phase of the War, as the Battle of the Marne had marked the first.

For us Riflemen the Ypres Salient must always be a sacred spot[2]—hallowed by the memory of the flower of the four Regular Battalions of the Regiment, who here laid down their lives for England—an abiding glorious thought!

The Regular Battalions—such as we knew them before the War—henceforth are no more: they must be reckoned as part of that "invisible army of heroic souls" whose name will live in the history of our race for all time. The reconstructed, re-equipped battalions, and the newly raised Service Battalions, inspired by the memory of their fallen comrades, and the record of their deeds, will doubtless follow in their steps, and will—please God—take part in the consummation of the final victory.

The Special Reserve Battalions.

On the outbreak of war the Cinderella of the Army, the Special Reserve, came into its own. Despised and rejected, this unfortunate branch of His Majesty's Forces had for many years struggled in adversity until the hot breath of War gave it new life, and the 5th and 6th Battalions, commanded by Lieut.-Colonel Richard Byron, D.S.O.,[3] and Lieut.-Colonel the Hon. John Roderick Brownlow respectively, were mobilised at Winchester upon the 8th August, 1914.

After the Regular Battalions had received their quota of Reservists, the remainder were drafted into the two Special Reserve Battal-

---

2. The area, over which the actual fighting took place, lies between the village of Gheluveldt and Hooge, on the Ypres-Menin high road, and is less than two miles in length by about 1000 yards in width.

3. Now brevet colonel, and commanding Infantry Brigade in East Kent. Succeeded by Lieut.-Colonel Guy St. Aubyn.

ions, who forthwith were moved to their allotted stations.

5TH BATTALION (SPECIAL RESERVE).

This battalion moved to Sheerness and the Isle of Grain, where a strenuous period of training and of equipping constant relays of reinforcements, combined with garrison duty in connection with the Thames defences, began. Up to the 31st December, 1915, reinforcements to the number of over 5000 officers and men were despatched to the battalions on service and a nucleus of 500 N.C.O.'s and men was provided in October, 1914, for the 14th Battalion as a supplementary Special Reserve.

The average strength of the battalion was approximately 2500.

6TH BATTALION (SPECIAL RESERVE).

This battalion reached Sheerness on August 9th, where, like the 5th Battalion, it has performed most valuable services in training officers and men, and in furnishing the Battalions on service with reinforcements. Up to 31st December, 1915, 5748 N.C.O.'s and Riflemen—including Rhodesians and Colonials, 244, and British Volunteers from Fiji, 99—have been sent abroad.

7TH AND 8TH BATTALIONS.

The narrative of the 7th and 8th Battalions, associated as they were from their earliest military existence in the same Brigade, is almost identical. Raised at Winchester towards the end of August, 1914, they were speedily moved to Aldershot, and placed under the Command of Lieut.-Colonel G. Rennie, D.S.O. (7th Battalion) and Lieut.-Colonel H. Green [4] (8th Battalion) respectively. Thanks to a sprinkling of officers from the Regular Battalions, and to a small but invaluable nucleus of N.CO.'s similarly transferred, the newly joined men made rapid progress in their training. It was not long, moreover, before they began to absorb the spirit and *esprit de corps* of Riflemen, which spirit was afterwards so gloriously displayed in the hour of their first fiery ordeal at Hooge in July of the following year.

These two battalions, together with the 7th and 8th Battalions of The Rifle Brigade, were formed at Aldershot into the 41st Brigade of Rifles—part of the 14th Light Division (Major-General Morland, C.B., D.S.O.[5])—under Brigadier-General F.A. Fortescue, C.B., whose

---

4. Now brigadier-general, and D.S.O.
5. Now Lieut.-General Sir Thomas L. N. Morland, K.C.B., D.S.O. Commanding an Army Corps.

administrative and organizing ability had ample scope in moulding this excellent material into a valuable fighting force. The early days of their training were beset with difficulties on every side, but tackled with energy and determination they were overcome, and in nine months from the date of formation, 18th May, 1915, the 41st Brigade of Rifles, then under the command of Brigadier-General O. S. Nugent, D.S.O., A.D.C to the king, left England for the more serious business overseas. In order that they should gradually become the better accustomed to the novel conditions of modern war, they were instructed in the art of trench fighting behind the lines, and it was June before they were moved up into the front line.

The 14th Light Division (then under *Major-General Victor Couper*) was selected to take part in the defence of the Ypres salient: a very high compliment to its efficiency. By a curious coincidence it fell to the lot of the 7th and 8th Battalions of the 41st Brigade, and to the 9th Battalion of the 42nd Brigade, to hold almost identically the same ground over which their gallant comrades of the four Regular Battalions had already so gloriously upheld the traditions of the Regiment, namely, the 1st and 2nd Battalions at the First Battle of Ypres, October 21st—November 13th, 1914, and the 3rd and 4th Battalions at the Second Battle of Ypres, April 19th—May 13th, 1915.

Writes a high and responsible staff officer:

For over six weeks, (June to July), the 14th Light Division held the trenches of the hotly-contested Ypres salient east of the Yser River upon the Menin high road, and had lost heavily every day from shell fire, when, upon the 21st July, the neighbouring Army Corps successfully exploded a mine in the German trenches close to Hooge, and occupied about 100 yards of the trenches on either side, which formed the apex of the salient.

Upon the following day the 41st Brigade was directed to move up and take over the defence of this place of honour, and to make it good. No sooner had the change been made than the enemy began a terrific bombardment, which served as a warning of the desperate counter-attack which followed. The salient of the position which had been seized was so situated that, although closely hemmed in by German trenches on three sides, it gave our men a strong tactical position, from which they could take the German front line of trenches on either side in reverse.'

It was obvious, therefore, to the brigadier in command that the recapture of the salient was a matter of utmost moment to the Germans, and he promptly made his dispositions with that idea, while warning the divisional general of the critical onslaught which he foresaw would come.

The 8th Battalion of The King's Royal Rifle Corps, under Green, and the 7th Battalion Rifle Brigade, under *Heriot-Maitland,* were allotted to the first line, and occupied the right and left lines of front and supporting trenches respectively. The 7th Battalion The King's Royal Rifle Corps and the 8th Battalion Rifle Brigade, under Rennie and *Maclachlan,* were in reserve.

The Germans maintained an uninterrupted bombardment, which resulted in a systematic destruction of the trenches by shell fire and by *minenwerfer.* At the end of a week there were hardly any trenches left, and the two battalions in first line, without sleep, and worn with constant watching by day and night, sorely needed a rest. The night of the 29th-30th July was accordingly fixed for their relief by the two battalions in Reserve, namely, 7th Battalion The King's Royal Rifle Corps and the 8th Battalion Rifle Brigade.

Hardly had the battalions exchanged places when, at 3.20 on the 30th, the Germans began a burning gas attack upon the front of the trenches we had captured from them ten days before, and at the same time a terrific shell and *minenwerfer* fire was opened on the support trenches. The German trenches were not more than twenty yards distant. What actually was the effect of the flame attack we do not know, as not a single man was left alive to tell the tale, except an officer's servant, who escaped by a miracle.

Meanwhile the Germans lifting their fire on to the woods, where the Reserve Companies were placed, assaulted in three columns. On two sides they were beaten off, but upon gaining the front trench they poured in and took the sector in reverse. Driven by the concentrated artillery and machine-gun fire, and pressed by the overwhelming numbers of the enemy, who were able to enfilade and take in reverse the supporting trenches as well as the front line, the position became untenable, and the remnants of the 7th Battalion in the front trenches fell back, and, rallying upon the outskirts of the Sanctuary and Zouave Woods, connected up with the Menin Road. Two Companies, however, under Wormald and La Terrière, continued to hold on to the trenches on the flank facing the Menin Road, where they maintained a gallant and stubborn fight until nightfall.

Reinforced at this point by the two battalions recently relieved, who without food, water, or sleep, had been rushed up from their short and hurried rest, the whole brigade were at last assembled, and able to hold their ground.

The brigadier-general in command early on the scene had grasped the situation. Recognising the immensely superior force of Germans, backed by an overwhelming artillery and machine guns, it was obvious that a counter-attack, under the existing conditions of open ground and with jaded troops, was impracticable. He urged that a large reinforcement to the extent of a complete division should be sent, and a lengthened bombardment by artillery superior to those of the enemy should be at once arranged, without which he viewed the chances of success for any counter-attacks as desperate.

The reply was an order to counter-attack at once, but yielding to further representation that two brigades were the minimum force required, a reinforcement of one battalion (Duke of Cornwall's Light Infantry) was sent, and the co-operation of another—9th Battalion The King's Royal Rifle Corps (Lieut.-Colonel Chaplin), of the 42nd Brigade— was promised along the Menin Road. A bombardment by the Corps Artillery was also arranged, which, beginning at 2 p.m., was to end at 2.45, upon which the counter-attack was to be delivered.

In for a frontal attack, as a desperate counter-stroke, there was not an officer or man who did not realize the situation and did not count the cost. The bombardment was ineffective, nevertheless the assault was launched at the appointed hour.

Writes an officer of tried experience in previous campaign:

We went at it—officers and all—as cheerfully and gallantly as ever we Riflemen did at Spion Kop, Talana Hill, or Delhi Ridges, but the odds were too great, and our forty-five minutes' bombardment had done nothing to save us There was not an inch of dead ground.

Writes the leader of the brigade:

Led by their officers, each successive line swept forward, and the last wave of men rolled forward from the woods with determined courage. The men literally fell in swathes, and headway was impracticable. First came a message from the left that one company only still remained. Shortly after, about 3.30 p.m., the senior officer on the right reported that further progress was impossible. It was clear that the attack had been pressed home

112

with a splendid gallantry and to its furthest limit, but that success was impracticable.

The brigadier—judging rightly that to further press his attack would be to sacrifice his whole brigade, and would be unjustifiable under the circumstances—directed his commanding officers to "incur no further avoidable losses, and to hold the edge of the woods till dark." Rallied at the confines of the Sanctuary and Zouave Woods, it was found that a bare remnant of 720 of all ranks could be mustered of the four thousand men of the brigade. July 31st. During the evening a respite occurred, but at 2.30 a.m. on the 31st the enemy renewed their attack. All through the day the 41st Brigade, reinforced by two additional battalions, held on until late in the afternoon, when it was withdrawn.

Wrote Brigadier-General Nugent:[6]

The curse of the salient had been heavy. . . . Our losses great. Officers of a class we shall never be able to replace, the pick of English or British Public School and 'Varsity life. Heroes in battle, they led their men with the most sublime courage, knowing, as I am certain they did, that they were going to certain death. The splendour of it! The glorious sacrifice of courageous lives in a noble cause! . . . There is nothing but praise for the conduct of these young battalions of The King's Royal Rifle Corps and the Rifle Brigade; nothing that you cannot relate with satisfaction and pride. They have had a fiery trial prolonged over nearly six weeks, culminating in the events of the 30th and 31st July, 1915, and they have acquitted themselves worthily of the best traditions of the two great Regiments to which they belong.

★★★★★

Alike sacred therefore must be the Ypres salient to all Riflemen of the Old and New Armies, and forever memorable in the Annals of the Regiment will remain the splendid services of the seven battalions. The area of ground on either side of the Ypres-Menin Road will be for the Regiment a doubly hallowed spot, wherein the heroic spirit of the Old Regiment blended with the spirit of eager patriotism of the New, and together showed a glorious example of self-sacrifice

---

6. Promoted major-general shortly afterwards to command the Ulster Division. C.B., and D.S.O.

and devotion to duty which can never be surpassed. (*Vide* "In Memoriam," 1st, 2nd 3rd, and 4th Battalions at the First and Second Battles of Ypres.)

******

Upon hearing of the trying ordeal through which the 41st Brigade of Rifles and 9th Battalion of the Regiment had passed, His Majesty the King, through Lord Stamfordham, was pleased graciously to allow the following extract of a letter to be conveyed to the brigade:—

Royal Pavilion, Aldershot,
August 22nd, 1915.

The King saw the 41st Brigade of Rifles here more than once, and remembers what a splendid body of officers and Riflemen it comprised. No one grieves more than His Majesty for the overwhelming and irreparable losses which it sustained during those eventful days.

Yours very truly,

Stamfordham.

For the remainder of 1915 the 7th and 8th Battalions performed the usual duties associated with trench routine warfare, but they did not take part in any important engagements.

Note.—The above narrative of the action at Hooge,[7] 29th-31st July, 1915, should be read in conjunction with the narrative of the 9th Battalion.

9TH BATTALION.

Formed on the same date as the 7th and 8th Battalions, the experiences of the 9th Battalion, under Lieut.-Colonel Charles Chaplin, during the early days of training in August, 1914, were August, similar in all respects. Having recently relinquished the command of the 3rd Battalion in India, Chaplin was well qualified to know what a Rifle Battalion should be, and he contrived, with the assistance of a small but valuable staff of veteran officers and N.CO.'s, and of an enthusiastic set of officers, to mould the 9th Battalion upon the lines of the 3rd Battalion, known in the eighties as the "Fighting Battalion." The period of training over—on the 20th May, 1915—the battalion

---

7. The editor is indebted to the editor of the *Regimental Chronicle* for permission to reproduce the account of this action, given in the edition for 1915 under the heading of "Trial by Fire": A Narrative of the *Baptême de Feu* of the 7th, 8th, and 9th Battalions.

left Aldershot for France with the 42nd Brigade (Markham[8]) as part of the 14th Light Division. The period of special Field Training was spent near the district of St. Eloi, and, having learnt their business, the Brigade moved with their Division to the notorious "Bloody Salient" at Ypres.

After nearly six weeks of the same trying experiences as the 7th and 8th Battalions in the 41st Brigade, the 9th Battalion had just been withdrawn into Reserve for a short spell of rest east of Ypres, when on the 30th July a sudden order came for it to co-operate upon the Ypres-Menin Road with the 41st Brigade in the counter-attack which had been ordered (*vide* Narrative of 7th and 8th Battalions). At noon, on the 30th July, the battalion, under Chaplin, marched accordingly to the given point of assembly on the Menin Road, close in rear of its own brigade holding their entrenchments. All necessary dispositions were then made before the covering artillery bombardment began, and at 2.45, after it had ceased, the attack was immediately delivered.

Comfortably rested and well fed, the battalion was in splendid fighting trim; inspired by a deep devotion to their colonel, in whom they had implicit confidence, the battalion was eager to distinguish itself. Preceded by its bombers, the two leading companies, namely, B (Tanqueray) and D (Durnford), each in two successive lines, punctually at 2.45 p.m. cleared the trenches held by their brother Riflemen of the 9th Battalion Rifle Brigade, and, rushing the intervening 200 yards, carried the enemy's trenches at the point of the bayonet. In the act of directing his men to make good their success, Chaplin[9] came under machine-gun fire and fell, shot through the head. Durnford and Tanqueray were also killed, and the command devolved upon Eric Benson. [10]

C Company (Young), next in succession, acting according to orders, moved diagonally to its right to cover the exposed flank of the

8. Brigadier-General, late The King's Royal Rifle Corps, *vide* chapter 9, C.
9. For an Obituary Notice of Lieut.-Colonel Charles Slingsby Chaplin, *vide Regimental Chronicle*, 1915. This gallant officer had won the affection and respect of his officers and men to a very remarkable extent. 'During the whole of my soldiering', writes (August 6th, 1915) the regimental-sergeant-major on behalf of the non-commissioned officers and private Riflemen, 'I have never served under happier conditions The battalion had not been long formed before the men respected and admired their colonel . . . . and gradually grew together as one large family with the same love for their dear colonel as sons would have for their father.'
10. This gallant officer was subsequently killed in 1916, while temporarily in command of the battalion.

two leading companies; a flanking enemy trench was then rushed, and in a spirit of bold initiative the company was again led forward by its captain in a further bayonet charge. This gallant effort would have led to important, if not decisive results, by relieving the pressure upon the flank of the 41st Brigade, as well as by supporting their own two companies. The main attack had however failed, and an overwhelming fire made further progress by C Company impossible.

Many had fallen, but the arrival of A Company (Exell) in support enabled the survivors to make good the trench already gained, and to hold their ground. The greatest gallantry was shown by the last-named company. Captain Exell himself went forward under a heavy fire into the open and brought in Captain Young of C, who was badly wounded; when going out again to assist a private Rifleman he was mortally wounded. Many other acts of heroism and self-sacrifice occurred by men striving under a murderous fire to rescue their wounded comrades lying in the open. Major John Hope,[11] second in command, was also wounded at the same time.

Great as were the losses, the survivors felt that they had done justice to the leading of their gallant chief, and shewn themselves worthy of the best traditions of their Regiment.

Oliver Nugent, commanding 41st Brigade, in writing of the gallant efforts and steadfast courage of his own Riflemen during the unsuccessful counter-attacks, was able to add in chivalrous and characteristic terms that his old friend and comrade:

> Chaplin was killed most gallantly leading his battalion His Riflemen did even better than mine, because they came up in the flank, and did recover some of the trenches on our left, which we had to evacuate, when they were outflanked by the centre giving way in consequence of the liquid-fire attack and overwhelming onslaught of the enemy.

The loss of the battalion in this short action was 17 officers and 333 other ranks. *Vide* In Memoriam, 7th, 8th, and 9th Battalions.

The battalion took no further part in any important fighting until the Battle of Loos on September 25th, where they again experienced very hard fighting, lost heavily, but won further credit for their gallant services. During the remainder of the year until 31st December the battalion took no part in any fighting incident of importance.

---

11. Now Lieut.-Colonel John Hope, D.S.O., M.P. *Vide* 19th Reserve Batallion.

Note.—The narrative of the 9th Battalion should be read with that of the 7th and 8th Battalions.

10TH AND 11TH BATTALIONS.

The formation of these two battalions followed rapidly on the heels of their predecessor of the New Army, and, in fact, their nucleus consisted of the surplus requirements of the 7th and 8th Battalions. The middle of September, 1914, found them with an administrative staff and organization of their own, and respectively commanded by Colonel W. S. Kays[12] and Lieut.-Colonel W. H. L. Allgood.[13] The former was soon promoted to command the 51st Brigade, and was succeeded by Lieut.-Colonel F. Douglas Pennant,[14] who was in command when it embarked.

To dwell on the vicissitudes of their early career is unnecessary; it is sufficient to say that, under the tuition of these experienced commanding officers, Lieut.-Colonels Douglas-Pennant and Allgood, their efficiency had reached a high standard by the date (July 21st, 1915) when they received orders to embark for France, forming part of the 59th Brigade.

Their probationary period in trench warfare was uneventful until September 25th, when they were present at the Battle of Loos, but did not actually take part in the advance. Throughout the remainder of 1915 these two battalions worked hard, and won an excellent reputation, reflecting the highest credit on those responsible for their training. Although never having the good fortune to take part in any general action to 31st December, 1915,. they showed on all occasions that fighting spirit and devotion to duty which are the characteristics of the Regiment.

12TH BATTALION.

The 12th Battalion was formed a few days after the 10th and 11th Battalions.

In the first few months of its existence it was commanded by Lieut.-Colonel Hon. E. St. Aubyn,[15] followed by Lieut.-Colonel C

---

12. Now brigadier-general, late The King's Royal Rifle Corps, and M.I. *Vide* p. 69, and chapter 9, C.
13. Now brigadier-general (15th April, 191G), late The King's Royal Rifle Corps, and M.I.
14. Late The King's Royal Rifle Corps.
15. Lost at sea, when employed as Queen's Messenger in 1916. Late The King's Royal Rifle Corps, and M.I.

Ashburnham,[16] and finally by Lieut.-Colonel A. L. Paine, [17] C.M.G., D.S.O.; it completed its training in the neighbourhood of Aldershot and Salisbury Plain, and sailed for France on July 22nd, 1915, forming part of the 60th Brigade under the command of *Brigadier-General J. W. G. Roy.*

The battalion commenced its instruction in modern field requirements at Fleurbaix, being attached to the 8th Division, and was present at the Battle of Loos on September 25th, holding the front line, but did not take part in the actual fighting.

The battalion remained in this neighbourhood until December 14th, when it was directed to hold the front line trenches east of the Fromelles Road. During the first six months on active service the 12th Battalion had no opportunity of showing their fighting value, but it earned a high reputation for efficiency generally.

13TH BATTALION.

The steady flow of recruits from the Rifle Depot enabled the 13th Battalion to be formed at Winchester on October 7th, 1914, under the command of Lieut.-Colonel A. Blewitt,[18] and was shortly afterwards moved to the training ground near Tring. This unit comprised part of the 63rd Brigade of the 21st Division, at that time commanded by Lieut.-General Sir Edward Hutton. It commenced its training at Halton Park, Tring, and shaped so well that, on the occasion of his inspection of the division in November, 1914, it received a congratulatory message from His Majesty the King on its smart and soldier-like appearance.

In April, 1915, the battalion moved to Salisbury Plain, being transferred from the 63rd Brigade to the 111th Brigade, and came under the command of *Brigadier-General R. W. R. Barnes*, the divisional commander being *Major-General Count Gleichen*. Lieut.-Colonel A. Blewitt left the battalion on June 6th, and was succeeded by Lieut.-Colonel R. Chester-Master,[19] under whose command they sailed for France on July 30th, 1915.

In the vicinity of the famous wood, Ploegsteert, they first learnt the arts of trench warfare, and on September 2nd moved to Fonquevilles, taking over a line of trenches from the French.

The last three months of 1915 were occupied with plenty of hard work but no serious fighting, and in this hard school the raw material

---

16, 18 & 19. Late The King's Royal Rifle Corps.

17. Late The King's Royal Rifle Corps and M.I.

of the 13th Battalion was quickly matured, and showed that, given an opportunity, the confidence of its original founders in its success would be more than justified.

14TH AND 15TH RESERVE BATTALIONS.

These two battalions were formed from the surplus establishment of the 5th and 6th Battalions (Special Reserve) in November, 1914, and were placed under the command of Lieut.-Colonel Guy St. Aubyn[20] and Colonel Sir Thomas Milburn-Swinnerton-Pilkington, Bart., respectively.[21]

The formation of these Reserve Battalions was the outcome of the obvious necessity to provide additional units for supplying the rapidly increasing number of Service Battalions with trained reinforcements.

They were formed at Westcliff-on-Sea, and were later moved to Seaford, close to Newhaven, where they were provided with the necessary staffs for producing thoroughly trained and well equipped drafts. Theirs was an unending toil, with no hope of reward, but they stuck grimly to their work, determined to meet the insatiable demand of the Battalions overseas for trained men. It is hoped that future historians of this War, when the final story is told, will not fail to do the work of the Reserve Battalions full justice.

In September, 1916, these two battalions were amalgamated and became the 16th Training Reserve Battalion under Lieut.-Colonel Petre, C.M.G., late Rifle Brigade.

16TH (THE CHURCH LADS' BRIGADE) BATTALION.

The moment War was declared, the Church Lads' Brigade came forward to take their share in the national emergency, and offered their services to their country. On August 7th, 1914, Field-Marshal Lord Grenfell, governor and commandant, placed the whole of the organization, which included at least 50,000 Cadets—recognised as such by the War Office—at the disposal of His Majesty's Government.

On September 2nd, 1914, the Army Council accepted the patriotic offer to raise a Service Battalion, and the 16th Battalion of the Regiment was thereupon brought to life. The command of the battalion was given to Lieut.-Colonel C. Kindersley-Porcher (late of the Coldstream Guards), but, owing to ill health, he was succeeded in July, 1915, by Lieut.-Colonel C Wild (late Coldstream Guards).

---

20. Late The King's Royal Rifle Corps.
21. *Idem.*

The early training of the battalion was carried out at Denham, Bucks, and later at Perham Down Camp, Salisbury Plain, where it formed part of the 33rd Division. It owed not a little of its efficiency to the fostering care and personal interest of Lord Grenfell. On the military side its general efficiency and attainments were marked as being of an exceptionally high standard: as regards the discipline while under training, it had a sheet clear of military crime. It was said of the Battalion that, at the request of the men themselves, each day opened and closed with a period for silent prayer, and the daily morning parade began with the recognised Church Lads' Brigade Service. On November 15th, 1915, the battalion sailed from Southampton for France, and landing at Havre, proceeded to Aire, where it learnt its first practical lessons in modern warfare.

So successful and popular did the formation of this Battalion prove, that immediately on their departure for France Field-Marshal Lord Grenfell undertook to raise a Second or Reserve Battalion. In the circular letter addressed to the clergy of England and Wales inviting recruits Lord Grenfell was able to say:

> I have inspected and taken leave of the 16th Battalion on its going to the Front, and I can say that it would be hard to find another Service Battalion so well set up, smart, and with so fine a record as to conduct—there having been absolutely no crime in the battalion—thus showing what Church Lads' Brigade training has done in the past when put to the test.'

It is hardly necessary to add that this appeal met with enthusiastic response, and a Reserve Battalion was formed accordingly.

The subsequent narrative of the 16th Battalion: its steadfastness in days of stress, its fine soldierly spirit, and its gallantry in many fights, will be told in a future edition.

17TH (THE BRITISH EMPIRE LEAGUE) BATTALION.

Thanks to the public spirit shewn by the gentlemen who formed the Council of the British Empire League, our 17th Battalion was raised on the 21st of April, 1915, and Lieut. Colonel L. Whitehead, late of the 1st (V.B.) Surrey Rifles, was appointed to command.

Recruits were not plentiful, and it was not until the 1st of September, 1915, that the four companies were completed. They commenced their training at Hursley Park, Winchester, and completed it at Aldershot and Witley. In December Lieut.-Colonel L. Whitehead relinquished the command of the battalion, and was succeeded by Lieut.-Colonel E. F. Ward.[22] Its subsequent history belongs to a period not covered by this edition.

18TH SERVICE (ARTS AND CRAFTS) BATTALION.

It was to Sir H. H. Raphael, Bart., M.P., that the 18th Battalion owes its creation. Sir Herbert, although fifty-six years old, had set a wonderful example to younger men by joining the 24th Battalion of the Royal Fusiliers as a private. After reaching the rank of captain, he was commissioned to raise the 18th Battalion on June 7th, 1915. He was entirely successful in his efforts, and on September 4th the War Office officially took over the battalion with a strength of 10 officers and 900 other ranks, and Lieut.-Colonel G. A. J. Soltau-Symons[23] was appointed to command. Their training was carried out at Gidea Park, Witley, and Aldershot.

Their history from 1st January, 1916, will be recorded in a future edition.

19TH RESERVE BATTALION.

Formed in October, 1915, from the Reserve Companies of the 16th and 17th Battalions, the 19th Reserve Battalion was first commanded by Lieut.-Colonel E. Kelly Purnell, and later by Lieut.-Colonel J. A. Hope, D.S.O., M.P.,[24] from the 9th Battalion, and afterwards by Lieut.-Colonel R. D. Keyworth. This battalion therefore, from being the offspring of the 16th and 17th Service Battalions, became their foster mother, and a steady flow of well trained and disciplined recruits was the result.

THE RIFLE DEPOT.
From 5th August, 1914, to 31st December, 1915.

The Rifle Depot at Winchester, with its Headquarters and Permanent Staff together with the Regular officers attached to the 5th and 6th Battalions of The King's Royal Rifle Corps, and the 5th and 6th Battalions of the Rifle Brigade, was under the command of Colonel (now Brigadier-General) F. A. Fortescue, C.B., late commanding 4th Battalion The King's Royal Rifle Corps, when War was declared. The whole of the mobilization work was carried out under his direction and personal supervision with admirable result. The system created

---

22. Late The King's Royal Rifle Corps
23. *Idem.*
24. *Idem.*

during the South African War by Colonel Horatio Mends,[25] assisted by the late Major Riley, had since been continued by a succession of experienced commanding officers, and was admirably developed by Colonel Fortescue, assisted by Captain Judge, so that it again proved a complete success upon a vastly greater scale than in 1899-1902. The 4,353 Regular Reservists and 800 Special Reservists upon joining were clothed, armed, equipped, and sent to their War Stations between August 5th and 9th without a hitch. Later, in August, Colonel Fortescue left the Depot to take Command of the 41st Brigade of Rifles of the New Army, and was succeeded early in September by Colonel Viscount Hardinge, C.B., A.D.C. to the King, late Rifle Brigade, who has remained in command ever since.

The vastly responsible work carried out by the commandant and staff of the Rifle Depot from the early days of the War, and the important services that it has rendered to our Regiment and to our comrades of the Rifle Brigade, can only be fairly gauged at the end of the present crisis, when a full record can be supplied.

---

25. Now brigadier-general, and C.B. *Vide* "Rifle Depot," end Chapter 10.

PART 5

A Retrospect

The Regiment from its inception has possessed certain distinctive characteristics which are pre-eminently those required for making Light Infantry and Riflemen of the best type.

Raised in 1755, and inspired by the genius of Henry Bouquet, it early displayed that strong individuality, that self-reliant courage, and that ready initiative coupled with steady discipline, which won from the intrepid Wolfe himself the proud motto of *Celer et Audax*. In 1797, under the experienced command of Baron de Rottenburg, the famous 5th Battalion (Rifles) was raised as a special type of Light Troops, thus reviving those special qualities of the Royal Americans which had rendered the Regiment so renowned in its earlier years, and which won imperishable fame throughout the Peninsular War.

After a long interval of peace the Regiment, from 1836 to 1854, received a similar impetus at the hands of Molyneux and Dundas, and reaped a rich harvest of lasting honour and glory upon the Delhi Ridge by displaying the same supremely valuable characteristics which had distinguished it in America and in Spain. Again, from 1861-1873, under Hawley's commanding influence and inspiring skill, the Regiment, through the 4th Battalion, opened up a more rapid and elastic system of drill and tactics, a more intelligent treatment of the soldier, and the betterment of his life in barracks, of which the good effects are felt today not only in the Regiment but in the Army at large. The qualities thus maintained for a century and a half have borne in later years abundant fruit, of which the stubborn courage at the Ingogo fight, the calm discipline of the *Warren Hastings*, the eager valour of Talana Hill, and the impetuous assault up the slopes of the Twin Peaks are glorious examples.

To the same special qualities was due the inspiration which created the system and principles of the Mounted Infantry, and it is to the officers and men of the 60th that the inception and success of that valuable force is largely due.

Let the Riflemen now serving, who read of the deeds of their gallant comrades of the past, and of the splendid valour and glorious self-sacrifice of their comrades in the early phases of the present war—the greatest and the most fateful war of all time—remember that, if they are to maintain the traditions, and increase still more the reputation of the famous corps to which they belong, it can only be by cultivating the same spirit of ready self-sacrifice and unsparing devotion to duty, and by developing the same prompt initiative, steady discipline, and unflinching courage, which have ever been the secret of the Regiment's success.

Let each Rifleman also recollect that a distinguished past is rather a reproach than a glory unless maintained by an equally distinguished present, and developed, if possible, by an even more distinguished future.

www.ingramcontent.com/pod-product-compliance
Lightning Source LLC
Chambersburg PA
CBHW031858090426
42741CB00005B/545